You Get What You Get

*Break the Cycles You Didn't Choose,
Reclaim Your Identity, &
Create a Life That Finally
Feels Like Yours.*

Dawn M. Rivers

DAYBREAK YOGA LLC

LCCN: 2026911368

ISBN: 979-8-9958808-1-3 paperback, 979-8-9958808-0-6 ebook, 979-8-9958808-2-0 hardcover

Subjects: SELF-HELP / Personal Growth / Self-Esteem, SELF-HELP / Personal Growth / Happiness

First Edition

Cover design by: Keaf Holliday, Creative direction by: Dawn M. Rivers, Interior design by: Dawn M. Rivers

Praise for You Get What You Get

"Dawn beautifully names what so many women experience but rarely articulate: the realization that while our stories may differ, we often carry the same inherited patterns. This book is for women ready to break those cycles and embrace midlife as a sacred opportunity to reclaim their identity, honor their lived wisdom, and choose themselves unapologetically. It's both a mirror and a pathway forward."
— **Ylonda Rosenthal-Greene** E-RYT 500 Yoga Teacher. Entrepreneur. Musician & Sound Artist.

"In a world that often celebrates performance over authenticity, Dawn Rivers challenges women to pause, reflect, and reclaim their true identity. You Get What You Get is especially powerful for high-achieving women who are ready to break cycles and redefine leadership on their own terms. Dawn's voice brings clarity, wisdom, and a refreshing perspective to this important conversation."
— **Tenora Edwards, Hon.D.Ent., M.S.**

"Nothing brings vision into focus like true vulnerability. Dawn has so authentically bared open her own life, those of us reading will not only learn something, but we'll feel the empathy she has for each of our journeys. It's that empathy which makes her so good at what she does and it's that authenticity that makes this book such a good read. If you are looking for growth and impact, you are in the right place."
— **Marissa Nance** Founder & CEO, Native Tongue Communications

"This book is for high-achieving women who are tired of performing a life that no longer feels like theirs. Dawn bridges personal story with practical insight, showing how identity patterns are formed and how they can be broken. A powerful guide for any woman ready to stop repeating cycles and start living with intention."

— **Sanaa Jaman, Ph.D., MBA** International Yoga Teacher & Studio Owner

"You Get What You Get is a deeply powerful and personal testimony that generational trauma can be stopped in its tracks. Rivers' book is a gift to the women who want to be free of dysfunction, pain and generational hurt. You won't be the same after reading this book."

— **Tara Pringle Jefferson** Author, Bloom How You Must: A Black Woman's Guide to Self-Care and Generational Healing

"Dawn's work speaks directly to those in the midst of midlife who feel the quiet pull for something more honest, more aligned, and more their own. This isn't surface-level self-help. It's a deeply personal and reflective journey that invites readers to examine who they've been, release what no longer fits, and step into who they're becoming with clarity and courage. What sets this book apart is Dawn's voice. As a former yoga teacher and life coach, she doesn't position herself as someone with all the answers, but as someone who has done the work. That lived experience is woven into every page, creating a sense of trust, relatability, and grounded wisdom. For anyone navigating transition, identity shifts, or the question of what now, this book offers both a mirror and a path forward."

— **Keisean Raines** The Calm Coach: Wellness Consultant, Certified Peer Support Specialist, Facilitator, and Community-Based Wellness Leader

"It's one thing to theoretically understand subconscious behavior and the impact of generational trauma, it is another to be a living testament to the work it takes to diligently journey and heal the behaviors you have embodied. From the very first paragraphs, I was gripped as Dawn brought me into her journey. Through her own story and supporting coaching frameworks, this book will lovingly lead women who are ready to recognize and shift narratives of scarcity and unworthiness for themselves

and for their legacy. Dawn's authority as an academic, wellness professional, and life coach shine on the page as she invites the reader into this legacy work. This text is an invitation to ask hard questions, sit with the discomfort that truth can reveal, and choose to grow anyway."

— **Nike Olabisi-Green** MBA, Life Coach

"What I love about this book and the work within it is how it brings truth without judgment. It helps you see what's been running underneath and gives you a way to move differently. This is powerful, needed work."

— **Annette L. Hollimon Founder**, Forever Phoenix. Medical Reiki Master Teacher & Wholistic Practitioner.

Foreword

From the opening phrase, "My mom has been unhappy all of my life. That is not hyperbole. It is fact," I was jarred and couldn't wait to be drawn further into the story. To know the author, her mom and her stepdad piqued my curiosity. I wanted to read more.

While this book is a Memoir, it is also a guide for women, particularly midlife women, to understand how they got to this point in their lives. Many midlife women begin to look behind them believing the best part of them is in the rearview mirror, and the road ahead is shrinking.

Three years ago, when I met Dawn in the virtual world we created for ourselves I knew she seemed familiar to me, and as we began to talk I realized she was my former boss, John Lenear's daughter. I worked as a reporter and editor for The Call and Post Newspaper for a decade and recalled stories of Dawn's success, as well as conversations with her mom. We were just coming out of the Pandemic, and I wanted to complete my goal of re-establishing my Marketing & Public Relations business and completing a novel I started during the quarantine phase of the pandemic.

After our initial Discovery Call, it was clear we were a match and I am so grateful to her for the lessons I learned about myself and how to navigate a full life and be successful.

As I read this book the interconnectedness of her life and her business was masterfully presented. The storytelling is much like that of Isabel Wilkerson in *The Warmth of Other Suns*, one of my favorite non-fiction works. The style of writing is conversational yet deliberate at times, drawing the reader into the story much like a novel. The transitions from story to theory are smooth and seamless. This style allows the reader to enjoy what they are reading while also learning.

The skill with which it is written is not surprising, because as a former librarian and a lifelong lover of books she has learned from the best. Research and learning I would say are among her favorite pastimes, next to Yoga and traveling the world.

Why do you need to know that? Because as they say today, she has **receipts.** She is transparent about the traumas she experienced as a daughter and wife and her heartfelt desire to end the cycle.

You Get What You Get: Break the Cycles You Didn't Choose, Reclaim Your Identity, and Create a Life That Finally Feels Like Yours," is a love story she has written for women, particularly Black women and most importantly for herself. She has researched, tested and mapped out the plan for each of us to better understand the dynamics driving our psyche.

As I thought about what to write, part of my brain kept returning to the Bible. In Genesis we learn that we are made in the image of God. Some may say well yes, I know that - but my question to those people would be have you really processed what that means? The more I learn the heavier that knowledge becomes for me, because if I was created in his image that's a lot of pressure to please Him as I live my life. Much like how we feel growing up in the shadow of our parents. If the memories were good, we were always working to please them and make them proud. If the memories were challenging, we also wanted to please them but for very different reasons.

Understanding these dynamics and how they manifest themselves is key to this book. When I said Dawn had receipts I meant it, only someone with personal knowledge could write of her mother's many illnesses brought on by, "..a heart that has carried too much for too long." Sit with that for a few minutes and imagine women in your life – the sisters, friends, aunties that are gone too soon because they carried the burdens of so many.

As I said I knew her family and many of the revelations in this book were startling, proving to me that we never truly know what happens behind closed doors. It also illuminates the power of masks. I knew John for a decade and spent countless hours with him talking about writing, computers, politics and so much more but the man she describes in many ways was unknown to me, yet in hindsight I recognized him.

Understanding where we came from has been a rallying cry of Black Americans since January 23, 1977, when *Roots* first aired. This work examines ancestry and how more than DNA connects us to our past. Fortunately, Dawn was familiar with some of her family history as she sought to understand her mom, and how historical events helped to shape her life.

Her mom experienced a life-altering trauma when Dawn was a young girl. Her biological father abandoned her with two young children resulting in her initial traumatic experience. One that left her with long-term emotional problems.

While traumatized she was also operating as a "Strong Black woman," who needed to take care of herself and her children, so she left the south and headed to Cleveland. This is a pattern that Dawn would later repeat.

Finding herself unhappy, Dawn began her path to healing. As she said, "There was a moment–the moment I recognized I was dealing with two fools–when everything crystallized." This was the moment she began breaking the cycle and unknown at the time she began her path to healing and writing the masterplan for a successful program for herself and the countless other women seeking to find freedom and validation in their lives.

The plan started with the *Mindset Makeover,* followed by *Awakening the Light,* graduating to *The Awakened Woman Academy* and ultimately became The Luxe Identity Spiral.™ This is not an overnight program. Using her life as an easel and studying the emotional and scientific aspect of these emotions on clients it took more than five years to develop a process that works on many levels.

If you're ready to unlock the meaning of your identity, continue reading and share it with a friend. This is a journey that so many women need to take, let's not harness this transformative experience alone.

Congratulations Dawn, I wish you nothing but peace and happiness as you continue to evolve into the precious gem you were meant to be.

With love,
Shelley M. Shockley
Owner & Principal Creative
Shelley M. Shockley Communications

For my mom.

And for the woman who is the mother, daughter, sister, aunt, cousin, godmother —
who lost her identity along the way. This book is for you. Your life can be happy, whole,
and free. You are a **Luxenary**, a visionary of your own becoming. You are seen. And
you always were.

"The way of fools seems right to them..."
— Proverbs 12:15

"I wasn't confused. I was committed."

Contents

Introduction — 1

MY MOTHER'S HEARTBREAK BECAME MY BLUEPRINT

How to use this book — 4

1. TWO FOOLS (THREE IF I STAYED) — 5

2. YOUR GRANDMOTHER'S PAIN IS LIVING IN YOUR BODY — 15

PART ONE — 26

3. YOU'RE NOT LAZY. YOUR NERVOUS SYSTEM IS EXHAUSTED. — 27

4. YOU'VE READ EVERY BOOK. WHY ARE YOU STILL HERE? — 38

5. THE WOMAN SHE PRAYED YOU'D BECOME — 52

PART TWO — 64

Your truth needs practice, not permission. — 65

6. YOU'VE BEEN LYING TO YOURSELF AND CALLING IT KINDNESS — 66

Your rituals are reminders of who you're finally becoming. — 78

7. YOUR MOTHER NEVER RESTED. THAT STOPS WITH YOU. — 79

Your body tells the truth long before your words do. — 91

8. STAND UP STRAIGHT. YOUR ANCESTORS ARE WATCHING. 92

Change your breath; change your frequency. 103

9. SHE SMOKED TO COPE. YOU'RE GOING TO BREATHE INSTEAD. 104

Stillness is intelligence, not emptiness. 114

10. YOU WERE RAISED ON NOISE. NOW YOU HAVE TO LEARN QUIET. 115

Whatever you place your attention on becomes your future. 126

11. YOU CAN'T DRIVE FORWARD LOOKING IN THE REARVIEW MIRROR 127

Presence is the ultimate luxury. 138

12. YOU'VE BEEN SHOWING UP. NOW TRY ACTUALLY ARRIVING. 139

Peace is the woman who stops abandoning herself. 150

13. THE DAY I STOPPED TRYING TO SAVE HER AND STARTED SAVING MYSELF 151

PART THREE 164

14. WHEN ONE WOMAN HEALS, A WHOLE FAMILY SHIFTS 165

15. NOW THAT WE KNOW BETTER 183

Saying goodbye 197

Epilogue 198

Afterword 202

You get what you get because you get who you are

Acknowledgements 204

Notes 206

Introduction

MY MOTHER'S HEARTBREAK BECAME MY BLUEPRINT

My mom has been unhappy all of my life. That is not hyperbole. It is fact.

I grew up watching sadness take root in my mother's body. The truth is, I cannot remember her at a field hockey game, a choir concert, or a church activity from fifth grade through my senior year of high school. She signed me up for dance lessons and even made me take the bus to the local community college for classes, but I only remember her attending one recital. My senior year, I performed in a show choir; I was one of the dancers, yet she never came to a single performance.

What I do remember is her bed.

Her silence.

Her sadness.

By the time I reached high school, she was in church more often, searching for answers, searching for healing, searching for something she could not name. I didn't have the language back then, but my mother was battling depression. And she battled it quietly, privately, and alone.

My stepfather died when she was fifty-nine. Her world collapsed. Her grief and fear became so heavy that she lost the ability to walk without a cane for nearly a year. She developed fibromyalgia. Diabetes. A long list of ailments that often accompany a heart that has carried too much for too long.

But eventually she found something that brought her joy again. The Red Hat Society. A group of vibrant women who celebrated life, dressed boldly, and traveled together. She blossomed with them. I even attended events with her a few times. My children and I were proud of her. We celebrated her seventieth birthday in New York City and took her to a Broadway musical. I still remember her smile. She was radiant.

Two months later, everything changed.

She called me at work and said she heard something "pop" inside her head.

Something was wrong with her vision. My son, Brenton, was working as a substitute teacher in the same school building. We drove straight to her house. He took her to the emergency room while I followed behind, terrified. I slept on the cold ER floor for three nights while doctors ran test after test trying to determine what had happened.

An aneurysm.

An ocular stroke.

A shift in her vision that would change the trajectory of the rest of her life.

She was encouraged to go to a rehabilitation facility to regain skills and build a new way forward. She refused. She wanted to go home, even though home could not give her what she needed. And once she returned, she gave up on life entirely. She refused help. She refused antidepressants. She refused support. She refused to tell anyone because she feared being judged.

Seven months later, after an occupational therapist stole from her and betrayed her trust, I moved into her home. And living with her again felt like stepping back into my childhood. The sadness. The withdrawal. The emotional absence. The heaviness that lingered in every room.

Her refrain was the same every day.

"I just want to die."

For nearly a decade, she refused to accept help or participate in her own healing. She was never paralyzed. Never lost her speech. She simply brushed off help or consistently participate in her own healing. In her mind, her stroke was a death sentence. For me it became a constant, exhausting battle.

During the pandemic, the weight of caring for her broke something open inside me. I felt anger, resentment, grief. I reached out for therapy, but my hospital network was overwhelmed. My best friend recommended her therapist, Ms. Janice, and I finally found support.

She gave me one assignment that changed everything.

She said, "Ask your mother when she was last happy."

One afternoon, after taking my mother to get her hair done and treating her to lunch, I told her she looked pretty. She disagreed and listed everything she believed was wrong with her appearance. To shift the moment, I asked the question.

When were you last truly happy?

Her answer stunned me.

She said the happiest time of her life was when she was pregnant with me. My brother was a toddler. She was living with my dad's parents while he attended college in another state. She trusted him. She believed in their marriage. But then she began hearing stories about his infidelity. Her heart shattered.

My grandmother, her mother-in-law, loved her unconditionally. She begged my mother to stay with them. And my mother loved her deeply. But heartbreak can drown out even the strongest support. She went back home to her own mother, hoping my dad would come after her. He never did.

She moved to Cleveland with two small children, carrying grief, regret, and disappointment that had never been healed. She lived a life shaped by one unresolved heartbreak.

When I heard her story that day, something clicked inside me. My mother never recovered from the pain of that era. She regretted leaving the only place where she felt loved, supported, and safe. She spent the rest of her life trying to survive the sadness she never allowed herself to heal.

I also realized something else.
I had inherited her story.
And I was living it.

HOW TO USE THIS BOOK

A guide to reading with intention

EACH CHAPTER CONTAINS

- **Opening Narrative** Dawn's personal story that grounds the theme

- **Inherited Blueprint** Where the pattern comes from in your lineage

- **Yogic Philosophy** The ancient principle that unlocks the lesson

- **Archetype Breakdown** See yourself in Stella, Serena, or Theresa

- **Pattern Recognition Box** Name what has been running in the background

- **Luxe Lifestyle Ritual** A practical practice to embody the shift

- **Reflection Prompts** Questions that go beneath the surface

- **Dawnism** One truth to carry with you

- **Affirmation** Words to anchor your new identity

You do not have to read this book in order.
But you may find that it reads you.

Chapter 1

TWO FOOLS (THREE IF I STAYED)

P*atterns don't disappear; they pass down. Like heirlooms nobody asked for.*

I followed the same invisible script my mother wrote, that her mother wrote, that somebody's mother before that wrote. I married a man who showed me exactly who he was long before we ever exchanged vows. He told me he wasn't ready to marry. I moved out. Then I let him back into my heart, over and over again.

After a couple of months of living together with our infant daughter, I drove four hours home alone and got a flat tire. With a baby in the car. A trucker stopped because I had a "Baby on Board" sign. Even then, I didn't see the truth.

I was repeating my mother's story. Note for note. Word for word.

When Brittany was two, we started planning the wedding. I found a dress at a consignment shop. My mom and I found a venue. We had announcements made. It was all set, until he called and said he wasn't ready. My heart broke.

I decided to move on with my life, with my career, and to a new state. But he came back and I said, "I am not doing this with you anymore unless we get married."

Four years from where this all began, and on the day we were supposed to marry at the courthouse, this man called and told me he didn't pick up the rings. Didn't get the marriage license. The day we were supposed to marry. I was stunned. I called my mom, expecting support. You know what she said?

"It's okay. I'll work it out. Just come to the courthouse." Basically, my mom said, "Marry him anyway."

She said it was best for my daughter. Best for my reputation. Best for the church community we lived in.

So I did it. Lord help me, I did it.

And I followed my mother's footsteps straight into years of abuse, infidelity, gaslighting, intimidation, and spiritual manipulation. They called it "submission." I call it soul assassination.

I stayed because she stayed. She stayed because her mother stayed. And her mother stayed because she didn't believe she had a choice.

This is how cycles are born. And this is how they continue. Until somebody says "enough."

The Moment Everything Shattered (and Everything Changed)

My daughter, Brittany, told me her cousin saw her father with another woman.

Something inside me shattered. And then something else awakened.

For months I was lost in confusion, denial, self-doubt. I was devastated and destroyed. This disbelief was all-encompassing. His family knew. His coworkers knew. Everyone knew. Everyone except me. Isn't that always how it goes?

That was my moment of truth: I was living the same unhappy life my mother lived. The same life my grandmother lived. The same life that would become my daughter's if I didn't do something different.

And I refused to pass it down again.

I filed for divorce. I devoured books. I set boundaries. Badly at first, but I set them. I changed my environment. I changed my mind. I changed my language. I changed my identity.

There was a moment when I recognized I was dealing with two fools. Him and his mistress. If I didn't do something about it, there would be **three** fools: him, her, and me. I had begun a study on fools in the Bible and noticed a pattern. A fool is not someone who lacks knowledge, understanding, or intellect. Instead, they willfully ignore, refuse to respond, or repeat what is harming them.

She would call and yell at me. He would call and yell at me. That's when everything crystallized. If I participated in the foolishness, it made me just like them. So I refused to argue. Refused to explain. Refused to participate in madness. Told both of them to stop calling me or I would take legal action.

I asked God for clarity and got it. That was the day I took my power back.

That moment broke the cycle.

This book is going to show you how I healed the fear, anxiety, people-pleasing, perfectionism, scarcity, and emotional patterns that lived in my lineage for generations.
And it's going to show you how to break your own.

Meet Searching Serena (She's Probably You)

If you are reading this, you might be where I was. You see the patterns. You feel the weight of them. You recognize that something is off in your life and in your lineage, but you are not sure how to break free without breaking everything.

That is the heart of the **Searching Serena** archetype.
Searching Serena is the woman who is always looking for the answer. She is smart, capable, and usually the one other people turn to for advice. She has read the books, taken the courses, watched the sermons, and highlighted the devotionals. Yet inside, she feels stuck between who she is and who she knows she could be.
She is not stagnant; she is in motion.
But the motion is often circular instead of forward.

Searching Serena is overthinking, overgiving, and overanalyzing. She is the woman who signs up for another program because she hopes this will be the one that finally unlocks everything.

She wants to be happy.
She wants to be free.
She wants to break the cycle.
But she will find a way to bring all the pieces of her healing together.

That was me for a long time.

I had already lived through my own share of trauma: an emotionally destructive marriage, betrayal, spiritual gaslighting, and a long line of generational pain that began long before my grandparents. I could see the patterns of unhappiness in my grandmother, my mother, and in myself. I knew I did not want to keep living like that. I just did not know what to do instead.

I remember telling myself, over and over, "I hate my life." I did not say it once. I said it for years.

If you resonate with that, if you have ever looked around at a life you built and thought, "Is this it?" you might be a Searching Serena, too.

The thing about generational patterns is that they trap us in searching mode. They tell us that happiness is out there somewhere: in the next relationship, the next job, the next city, the next degree, the next church, the next spiritual teacher. We want a solution that will come from outside of us because that feels safer than confronting what is happening inside of us.

But here is the hope.

You can be the one who breaks the cycle in your family.

You can be the one who stops choosing partners who repeat your parents' patterns.

You can be the one who refuses to pass trauma forward.

You can be the one who chooses healing instead of hiding.

You can decide, as I did, that you are no longer available for an unhappy life.

That decision does not instantly erase pain. It does not rebuild your life in a day. But it opens a door. It invites something new. It begins to shift your identity from the inside out. And that is where the spiral of transformation truly begins.

This book is written for the woman who is tired of searching and ready to start **becoming**. The woman who wants more than survival. The woman who suspects she was meant for joy, freedom, and purpose, even if no one in her family has ever modeled that.

If that is you, keep reading. You are not alone, and you are not broken. You are a Searching Serena on the edge of becoming something more.

THE PROMISE (AND WHY MY DAD WAS RIGHT ALL ALONG)

My own journey did not start with a neat framework or a polished brand. It began with a woman who was exhausted, overextended, and determined not to die unhappy.

On paper, I was successful. I became a librarian in 1998. It took me three colleges and six years to finish my undergraduate degree, and then another four years to earn my master's by the time I was twenty-eight. By then I was married and had two children. I loved being a librarian. I loved books, students, and the rhythm of school life.

And I always had a side hustle.

First, I helped people write research papers. Then I edited them. I called my little business **Daybreak Services**. My biological dad was an entrepreneur and encouraged me to create something that was my own. He was a dreamer in every sense of the word.

My dad, Thom Rivers, went to North Carolina A&T. He knew Jesse Jackson. He marched in student protests for equity in Greensboro. He was a member of Kappa Alpha Psi and had friends all over the world. As a kid, I watched him glide through Chicago traffic in an orange Mercedes, snapping his fingers and singing along to R&B/Soul music as we rode down the Dan Ryan. He wore full-length fur coats and sharp suits, cowboy hats and purple lizard-skin boots, and sometimes traditional African outfits. When he told stories, everyone leaned in. And he loved to give advice.

He owned a magazine. A sales and marketing firm. A shea butter business long before shea butter was mainstream. He traveled to West Africa, especially Ghana and Mali. They loved him there. He even received a chieftaincy title in Mali. His final dream was a restaurant called **Thom's Turkey**, opened in 2009 to share his famous smoked turkey with the world. People loved it. Two months later, he passed away. My stepmother, my brothers, Tommy and Billy, and my niece Alexa kept his dream alive for almost a decade.

Dad was a dreamer. And for years, I insisted I was not.

He would say, "You should be your own boss. You should have your own business." I would answer, "No, Dad, that is your dream, not mine. I like being a librarian and knowing when my money is coming."

But life has a way of circling back.

In 2021, I launched a crowdfunding campaign called **#DreamsToReality** through IFundWomen. One of my dad's favorite nieces, Gwen, made a donation and wrote, "Your dad is smiling down and cheering on you!" That message hit me like a wave. It was a full-circle moment. The daughter who said she did not want to be an entrepreneur had become one.

My life had already expanded far beyond the library. I had opened my own yoga studio. I trained women of color to become yoga teachers. I hosted retreats. I dreamed of branded yoga mats, a thriving coaching practice, a career as a flight attendant, and one day, a book that would help women globally.

It finally dawned on me. I am a dreamer, too. Just like my dad.

And as I broke my own cycles, women started asking me how I did it.

One cousin asked how I seemed so happy all the time. I told her the truth. I was not happy all the time. I simply made a conscious decision to become a happy woman. I went back through my life and traced what I had done, step by step, to get from a place of deep pain to a place of genuine joy.

There was a pattern. I changed my thoughts. I changed my words. I changed my mind.

By then, I was a yoga teacher and studio owner. I had created my own yoga teacher training manual that was steeped in the Eight Limbs of Yoga. We studied the Yamas and Niyamas. Deborah Adele's book was required reading. My trainees had to choose one principle and integrate it into their practicum. My teaching staff wove them into their classes. Those ancient teachings became the foundation of my first framework.

Yamas are ethical restraints; how we relate to the world. Niyamas are observances; how we relate to ourselves.

Without realizing it, I was living them: telling the truth, releasing what no longer served me, cultivating discipline, practicing contentment, and returning to self-study over and over.

What started as breaking my own cycle quietly became a framework to help others break theirs.

I read everything I could get my hands on. I watched televangelists like Joel

Osteen, T. D. Jakes, and Miles Monroe. Then I read Joyce Meyer's *Battlefield of the Mind* and my perspective shifted. She taught that what we say about our lives shapes what we believe. After that book, I decided to experiment. I started saying, "I love my life."

I wrote the words on sticky notes and posted them on my bathroom mirror, in my car, wherever I would see them. I made a list of forty-two things I wanted to do in my forty-second year. Simple things and bold things. One of the first items was to go to the movies by myself. When I was married, I wanted to go alone and my husband mocked me for it. He could not understand why anyone would want to go to a movie alone. Or maybe he was projecting his own guilt? Either way, I did not go then. On my list, I decided I would.

I went to movies alone. Dinners alone. Concerts and plays alone. At my mom's encouragement, I joined several Meetup groups and explored my city in new ways. I ate at restaurants across town. I went on a haunted hayride. I danced on stage with a local cover band. I tried things I never would have allowed myself to experience before.

At the end of that year, something miraculous had happened. I actually loved my life.

I declared it on Facebook. By then, people had been following my adventures without knowing the full story. They cheered me on. I never made a big post about separation or divorce, but I am sure they knew. What mattered was not their perception. What mattered was my transformation.

That list of forty-two things gave me wings. It gave me agency over my own life. It helped me discover who Dawn was outside of marriage and motherhood. I became courageous. I craved change. I decided to move. My son was headed to college. My daughter had graduated and was building her own life. I no longer needed to live in a particular school district. I could choose a neighborhood based on my needs.

I changed my job assignment. I chose a different grade level. I shifted the after-school activities I was involved in. I changed my mind about being "just" a yoga practitioner and stepped into becoming a yoga brand rooted in spiritual curiosity, resourcing women, and empowerment.

And then, in one powerful courtroom moment, I changed my name.

After eighteen months of delayed hearings, excuses, and missed court dates, we stood before the magistrate on December 31, 2012. He said this case would not go into the next year. As we finalized the divorce, I asked for one more thing. I wanted my maiden name back.

"My last name is Rivers," I said. "I was born a Rivers and I will die a Rivers. I want my name back."

The magistrate wrote it at the top of the decree, signed and sealed it. In that instant, I was legally and spiritually **Dawn M. Rivers** again.

The woman who once said, "I hate my life," had rewritten her story.

The frameworks that you will encounter in this book were born from these moments. They are not theory. They are lived. They are tested. They are the structure that emerged when I looked back at the chaotic spiral of my life and realized it was not chaos at all. It was a pattern.

And patterns can be taught.
Patterns can be shared.
Patterns can set other women free.

That is the promise of this work.

YOUR INVITATION FORWARD

Through years of coaching women, studying patterns, and walking through my own healing again and again, something deeper began to emerge. I noticed similarities in the breakthroughs. I noticed consistency in where women got stuck. I could see the same emotional spirals appear in clients who had never met each other. What I once believed were individual challenges became recognizable patterns. And those patterns eventually formed the roots of a complete system.

This book will show you the path I took and the early framework that grew out of my own transformation. But there is more. After working through my own

Soul Blueprint—a deep excavation of my patterns, purpose, and identity—a new structure revealed itself. It was deeper, more integrated, and more expansive than anything I had created before. It still lived on the foundation of the Path to the Awakened Woman, yet it reached into identity, lineage, emotional architecture, and lifestyle in a way I could not ignore.

It felt as if my life's work had been preparing itself in the background, waiting for the moment I was ready to see it. And this book is your introduction to that evolution. It is not the whole method, but it is the doorway.

During that time, I grieved the closure of my yoga studio. The grief was so heavy that I drifted away from yoga altogether. I unfollowed accounts. I unsubscribed from newsletters. I could not bring myself to practice. But my heart ached for my foundation because yoga had carried me through every major turning point of my life.

I started practicing in 1999 after seeing a yoga class on PBS. By the time I discovered Rodney Yee's VHS tapes at the public library, I was hooked. I spent three years practicing alone in my basement before joining a gym. That first class with a teacher changed everything. Hot yoga changed everything again. I became a karma yogi, then a desk yogi, cleaning the studio for free classes, learning, watching, studying. When I finally said out loud that I wanted to teach, my managers said they were waiting for me to recognize it.

Those early years were filled with tears on my mat. Release. Awakening. Letting go. I often stayed for back-to-back classes: sixty, seventy-five, ninety minutes at a time. Yoga became my sanctuary. My community. My safe place. My soft place to land. My spiritual mirror. My refuge.

So when yoga called me back after two years away, it saved my life a second time.

All of that—the ancient wisdom, the personal transformation, the patterns I witnessed in hundreds of women—became part of a deeper system that I will reveal to you later in this book. Consider this your introduction, your foundation, your first spiral upward.

By the end of this book, you will have tools to break your own cycles and create the life you deserve. And when you are ready, the complete method will be waiting for you.

Let's begin by recognizing where you might feel stuck, and where your next evolution is ready to unfold.

THE LUXE IDENTITY SPIRAL™

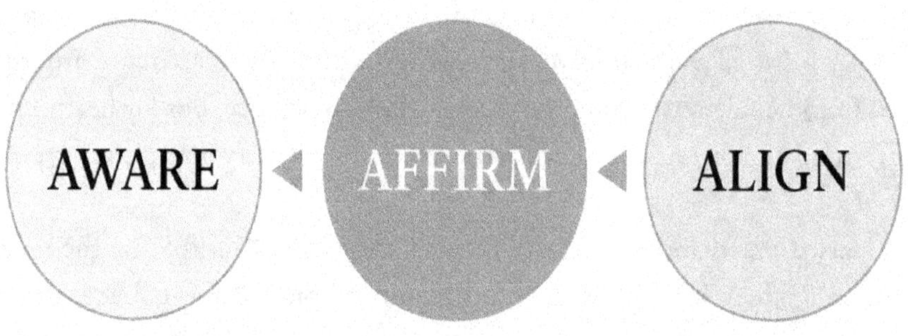

ROOTED IN THE EIGHT LIMBS OF YOGA

AWARE	AFFIRM	ALIGN
Yamas • Niyamas • Asana	Pranayama • Pratyahara • Dharana	Dhyana • Samadhi

You are not broken. You are becoming.

Luxe Identity Spiral

Chapter 2
YOUR GRANDMOTHER'S PAIN IS LIVING IN YOUR BODY

THE THREE VALIDATIONS: ANCIENT, PERSONAL, AND SCIENTIFIC

In 2012, I had no idea I was creating a framework. I was trying to survive. I changed my thoughts, my words, and my mind. I went from 'I hate my life' to 'I love my life.' I broke free from an 18-year abusive marriage. I stopped repeating my mother's patterns of unhappiness.

Ten years later, my cousin through marriage asked me a question that changed everything: "How are you so happy all the time?"

I paused. Was I happy all the time? No. But I had made a **conscious decision** to be happy. And somehow, it worked.

So I started reverse-engineering what I had done. What were the actual steps I took to get from drowning in generational patterns to living a life I loved?

For six months in 2022, I mapped it out. By then, I was a yoga teacher and studio owner, steeped in the Eight Limbs of Yoga, with a teacher training manual rooted in the Yamas and Niyamas. I knew exactly where to anchor the framework.

The Yamas and Niyamas had become the foundation of my teaching. I loved learning about them and sharing what I learned. So when I sat down to create a framework for the transformation I had already lived, I used them as my guide.

The Bluepring That Was Already There

Around 400 CE, a scholar named Patanjali compiled the Yoga Sutras: 196 short verses that outlined the path to freedom. He described Eight Limbs (steps) of yoga, and the first two limbs are called the Yamas and Niyamas.

The Yamas are ethical restraints, the "don'ts" that guide how we relate to others and ourselves. The Niyamas are personal observances, the "do's" that guide our inner life.

Here's the simple breakdown:

THE YAMAS (5 Restraints):
1. ***Ahimsa*** - Non-violence

2. ***Satya*** - Truthfulness

3. ***Asteya*** - Non-stealing

4. ***Brahmacharya*** - Non-excess/Moderation

5. ***Aparigraha*** - Non-possessiveness

THE NIYAMAS (5 Observances):
1. ***Saucha*** - Purity/Cleanliness

2. ***Santosha*** - Contentment

3. ***Tapas*** - Discipline/Heat

4. ***Svadhyaya*** - Self-study

5. ***Ishvara Pranidhana*** - Surrender to the divine

These weren't purely philosophical concepts to me. By 2022, I had been teaching them for years, watching them transform my yoga students' lives. I had seen how they worked on the mat and off.

So when I sat down to map my own transformation, these ancient principles became my blueprint.

Sanskrit Term	Simple Meaning	Luxe Identity Spiral™	Pattern It Breaks
— YAMAS (Ethical Restraints) —			
Ahimsa	Non-violence / Compassion	Speak to yourself with kindness	Self-criticism & inner cruelty
Satya	Truthfulness	Honor your real needs & desires	People-pleasing & silencing yourself
Asteya	Non-stealing	Stop stealing your own joy & time	Chronic sacrifice & self-neglect
Brahmacharya	Right use of energy	Invest energy in what builds you	Pouring from an empty cup
Aparigraha	Non-attachment	Release who you were told to be	Inherited identity & old roles
— NIYAMAS (Personal Observances) —			
Saucha	Purity / Cleanliness	Clear mental & emotional clutter	Generational noise & toxic patterns
Santosha	Contentment	Find wholeness now, not later	Conditional self-worth
Tapas	Discipline / Burning desire	Commit to your own becoming	Comfort zones & stagnation
Svadhyaya	Self-study	Know your Inherited Blueprint	Unconscious cycle-repeating
Ishvara Pranidhana	Surrender / Devotion	Trust your path and your healing	Control & fear-based living

The Yamas and Niyamas: ancient ethical principles reimagined as the foundation of the Luxe Identity Spiral™

Six Months, One Question, One Map

For six months, I worked on the framework. I looked back at my 2012 journey and asked: What actually changed? What were the core shifts that took me from inherited patterns to conscious freedom?

Three things emerged clearly:
My Thoughts. My Words. My Mind.

I had changed all three, and I realized each shift mapped directly to the Yamas and Niyamas I'd been teaching.

So I created what I called the **Path to the Awakened Woman** framework:

AWARE (Change Your Thoughts) - Based on Yamas:

- **Practice Peace** (*Ahimsa* - Non-violence) → I stopped the violent self-talk

- **Know Thyself** (*Svadhyaya* - Self-study) → I studied what made me happy

- **Contagious Contentment** (*Santosha* - Contentment) → I found gratitude in chaos

AFFIRM (Change Your Words) - Based on Both:

- **Honor Honesty** (*Satya* - Truthfulness) → I spoke truth and set boundaries

- **Sacred Sayings** (*Brahmacharya* - Non-excess) → I created non-negotiable self-care

- **Systematic Structures** (*Tapas* - Discipline) → I built consistent practices

ACTIONS (Change Your Mind) - Based on Niyamas:

- **Soothing Surroundings** (*Saucha* - Purity) → I cleaned up my environment

- **Count the Cost** (*Asteya* - Non-stealing) → I made informed decisions

- **Pack Light** (*Aparigraha* - Non-possessiveness) → I released what didn't serve me

SCIENCE FINALLY CAUGHT UP TO WHAT I ALREADY

KNEW

The research behind the transformation I lived before I understood it.

When I mapped my 2012 transformation in 2022, I realized I had changed my mindset. I had changed my biology. I had changed my brain. I had changed the patterns in my lineage. And none of it was accidental.

Everything I did intuitively, every breath, every affirmation, every yoga session, every moment of choosing peace, matched emerging scientific research in trauma, neuroscience, meditation, and epigenetics. As I dug deeper into the literature, what I discovered stunned me.

1. Epigenetics: Trauma Is Inherited, but So Is Healing

When I read about DNA methylation, I literally gasped. This wasn't metaphorical. My body had been keeping receipts.

I had thought I was carrying my mother's sadness and my grandmother's pain. Science now confirms this isn't metaphorical; it's biological.

Trauma doesn't change your DNA sequence. It changes how your genes are expressed, through something called DNA methylation. Think of it like sticky notes placed on your genetic code saying "turn this up" or "turn this down."

Here's what the research revealed:

- Trauma can alter gene expression across multiple generations

- Holocaust survivor offspring show measurable epigenetic differences

- A 2025 study on Syrian refugees found trauma markers in mothers, children, and even grandchildren

- Parents' experiences can influence the biological "stress settings" of their children

This means my mother's depression was emotional. It was epigenetic. My grandmother's pain was historical. It was biological.

But the most important finding that brought me to tears was this:

- Epigenetic changes are not permanent.

- They can be rewritten by our own life experiences.

Every yoga class, every affirmation, every breath, every moment of conscious choice was literally rewriting my lineage.

I was healing myself.

I was healing what I would pass down.

You feel that in your body right now, don't you? That recognition? That's your cells remembering.

2. Neuroplasticity: Your Brain Can be Rewired at Any Age

I didn't know the term "neuroplasticity" in 2012.

But I was living it.

Neuroplasticity is the brain's ability to reorganize itself: to form new neural pathways based on what you think, feel, repeat, and practice.

Meditation and yoga research now shows:

- Meditation increases cortical thickness

- Meditation reduces amygdala activity (fear center)

- Yoga practitioners show less age-related brain decline

- New habits create new neural pathways, literally reshaping thought patterns

I didn't know any of this. I only knew that the fog in my mind began to clear, the emotional pain loosened its grip, and my migraines and stress-related symptoms began to lift.

One meditation teacher told me, "However many years you spent in a traumatic relationship, expect at least that many years of meditation to fully release its imprint." This shocked me. I wanted a faster and easier way out of the pain and residual effects of it. But he was right. Over the years, the nightmares eased, the intrusive thoughts softened, and the inner tension unwound. Not magically, but neurologically.

My healing was not willpower. It was brain change.

3. Nervous System Science: Why Survival Mode Felt Like "Stuck"

For most of my life, my nervous system lived in a heightened state. Growing up in a household filled with emotional unpredictability made my body believe that danger could strike at any moment. I never really knew how my mother would react. She didn't trust me or anyone. She would show up at my high school or check to see if I was really at my friends' houses. My friends were always confused because they said, "Your mom is so strict, but you never do anything wrong." I felt the pressure to be perfect. I was in a heightened state of anxiety, and my body was suffering.

The constant headaches I had led my mom to take me to specialists to see if I had a brain tumor. I had scans and several appointments before the doctors determined there were no problems with my brain tissue. In the early 1980s, children and young adults weren't being diagnosed with stress or anxiety. They didn't address the sadness or fear I was experiencing.

Science now calls this sympathetic dominance: the fight-or-flight system stuck "on."

Trauma research reveals:

- Trauma disrupts the balance between fight-or-flight and rest-and-digest

- The body begins to release stress hormones even without real danger

- Chronic survival mode creates exhaustion, anxiety, numbness, and emotional shutdown

- Breathwork activates the vagus nerve, pulling the body out of survival and into safety

What I experienced as chaos, burnout, overwhelm, and emotional reactivity wasn't a personal flaw. It was a physiological response to long-term stress.

Yoga, breathwork, and mindfulness weren't "self-care." They were recalibrating my nervous system. They were shifting me from survival to safety. The very condition required for healing.

This is the biological foundation of the woman I call Stagnant Stella. She is not unmotivated. She is not disorganized. She is not lazy. Her nervous system is simply overwhelmed.

4. Affirmation Science: Why "I Love My Life" Wasn't Delusion. It Was Neurobiology

When I wrote "I love my life" on sticky notes over and over, I felt like a liar. I was still in pain. I was still in crisis. Doubt was ever-present. Depression was my constant companion. But something inside told me to keep going.

Affirmation research shows that repeating positive statements activates the brain's reward pathways, especially the ventromedial prefrontal cortex. The same area that lights up when something good actually happens to you.

Studies show:
- Affirmations improve emotional regulation

- They increase activity in identity and value-processing areas

- They can change behavior

- Most people feel shifts after 3–4 weeks

That was exactly my timeline.

What felt like "faking it" was actually training my brain to believe something new.

Every sticky note was a planting. Every repetition was a neural rehearsal. Every tiny shift was a sign that the old pathways were weakening and new ones were forming.

5. Black Women & Generational Trauma: The Context That Completed the Picture

As I learned more, I realized my story wasn't personal. It was cultural. I had heard it echoed in the stories of countless clients, students, and women I'd never even met.

Being a Black woman meant carrying not only my mother's and grandmother's wounds, but centuries of inherited pain. My grandfather had a second family and no longer wanted his current family. He tried to "get rid" of them, but my great uncle saved my grandmother, uncles, and mother before this became a reality. That pain has haunted our family for generations. Relatives don't speak about it or acknowledged how it affects them.

My great-grandparents were one generation from slavery and their white relatives lived across the road. My great-aunts spoke of their cousins who "passed" when they moved up north. My mother lived in the time when having a library card was illegal. They all experience the extreme ramifications of slavery, racism, and Jim Crow laws of the South.

Research on Post-Traumatic Slave Syndrome, emotional weathering, and racialized stress reveals:

- Chronic racism accelerates cellular aging

- Emotional coping strategies from slavery still show up in Black families

- "Strong Black Woman" is a survival adaptation that often prevents rest

- Harsh parenting patterns are sometimes rooted in historical protection strategies

- Cultural trauma impacts physical and mental health across generations

Understanding this didn't excuse behavior, but it contextualized it. It helped me see the bigger picture:

- I was breaking my *own* cycle.

- I was breaking a *cultural inheritance* of survival.

The science didn't weaken my faith. It strengthened it. I cried. Right there on the yoga studio floor. Because science was finally saying what my soul already knew. Thankfully, it showed me that God, yoga philosophy, trauma research, neuroscience, and ancestral resilience were all telling the same story:

Healing is possible.

Patterns can change.

You are not your past.

Your lineage can shift through you.

The research says trauma changes gene expression. What it means? Your grandmother's fear lives in your shoulders. Your mother's anxiety lives in your breathing. Their pain literally shaped your biology. But here's what made me shout: It's reversible.

WHAT THE RESEARCH CONFIRMED

Then something amazing happened. As I was finalizing my framework, I remembered reading books on neuroscience, like *Buddha's Brain* and others. During the pandemic, I held book discussions with my community. As I prepared to lead talks, I read related books and articles. This sparked a new understanding for me. New threads were created. Curiosity was cooking. So I dove into more research on meditation, neuroplasticity, and trauma.

And I discovered that science could now prove what I had done intuitively in 2012 and systematized in 2022 using ancient yoga philosophy.

When I changed my thoughts, my words, and my mind, I had a mindset shift.

I was literally rewriting my biology. And the part that brought me to tears?

Every time I practiced yoga, every time I said "I love my life," every time I chose differently, I was literally rewriting my genetic expression. I was healing myself. I was healing my lineage.

I spent six months on this framework because I wanted to get it right. I wanted to honor the ancient wisdom that had saved me while making it accessible to modern women breaking cycles.

What I had lived in 2012, I systematized in 2022.

What I didn't realize at the time was that my personal healing was only the beginning. Once I understood the scientific and spiritual truth behind my transformation, I could finally see the deeper pattern: the steps I took in 2012 weren't random acts of survival. They were the early architecture of a repeatable process: a way through.

And when I began coaching women, I watched that same process unfold again and again.

Different childhoods. Different wounds. The same inherited patterns. The same turning points. The same breakthroughs.

Over hundreds of conversations, private sessions, tears, revelations, and pattern-mapping, something became undeniable: there was a system to the healing journey. A predictable arc. A transformation sequence. A spiritual, emotional, and neurological pathway women were walking without knowing they were walking it.

What started as my story became a shared story. What began as an intuitive awakening became a teachable method. What healed one lineage revealed the blueprint for healing many.

This book is the foundation of that blueprint, not the entire system, not yet, but the doorway. The first step into understanding why you feel the way you feel, where your patterns come from, and how they shift.

Now that you understand why cycles repeat and how they can be rewritten, it's time to meet the women inside this work. The archetypes who show us where the healing begins.

The first one is the woman I was for years. The woman who senses there's more, but can't quite name what's missing.

Let me introduce you to Stagnant Stella.

PART ONE

AWAKENING

*This is where you see what
you can no longer ignore.*

Chapter 3
YOU'RE NOT LAZY. YOUR NERVOUS SYSTEM IS EXHAUSTED.

Stagnant Stella and the moment everything starts to make sense

The feeling of being stuck has happened to me more than once in my life. As a teenager, I didn't know what I wanted to do after graduation. I remember feeling lost, and the space between me and my best friends was getting wider. I started spending time with a new friend who seemed more adventurous than me, and she influenced me easily. We cut class together, went to the liquor store during school hours, and generally just wasted time.

I would go to homeroom and first-period class, then disappear until ninth or tenth period to avoid the assistant principal calling my home. I thought I was slick and getting away with something. Until my English teacher told me that if I didn't start coming to class, I would fail my senior year.

I had no idea I was on the verge of failing. I wasn't even having fun. You know how you can get too far into something to turn back, or at least you think you are. That was me. I was stuck, going through the motions. His warning felt like a lifeline pulling me out of the mud.

The only person I was fooling was myself.

It worked out in the end, but that decision stalled my life for almost a decade. I had to catch up by taking remedial classes in college. It was embarrassing to attend a university and pay full tuition only to be placed in remedial courses. Three years later, I earned an associate degree from that four-year institution. It ultimately took six years and three different colleges before I finally earned my undergraduate degree.

Looking back, teenage me was already living as a young Stagnant Stella, overwhelmed, directionless, influenced by others, and unable to see my own potential.

Stagnant Stella struggles every day to make decisions. For example, she might want to lose weight and tell everyone she's starting at the gym this month. But her schedule is packed with obligations, and she has no idea how to organize her life in a way that makes time for herself. She blames others for her inability to create healthy habits. She tends to move through the world sad, bitter, overwhelmed, and unsure how to break out of the cycle.

Stagnant Stellas are amazing individuals with big dreams, but negativity and self-doubt hold them back. She feels stuck, like she's wandering in a dense, dark forest. She is able to see the light through the trees but unsure how to reach it.

Every Family Has a Stella

Every family has a Stella. She is the woman who carries what no one else could name. She moves carefully, quietly, doing her best to keep the peace while holding the weight of generations on her back. Her life looks stable from the outside, routine, predictable, safe, but inside she feels like she's running in circles.

Stagnant Stella is not lazy or unmotivated; she is *over-conditioned.* She has inherited beliefs that whisper, *Don't ask for more. Don't make a scene. Don't outshine anyone.* She learned early that survival depends on staying small. These lessons didn't begin with her; they were passed down like family heirlooms from women who endured betrayal, scarcity, or emotional neglect.

Generational patterns doesn't always roar. Sometimes it hums. It shows up as hesitation before opportunity, guilt after success, or silence when truth wants to rise. Stella's patterns are protection spells from her lineage, created by women who didn't have the privilege of safety or choice. Their caution became her cage.

In Stella's world, self-sacrifice is love. Overworking feels like worth. Rest feels undeserved. She tells herself she's being responsible, but deep down she's afraid that change will make her disloyal to the women who came before her. That is the heartbreak of generational cycles. It binds devotion to limitation.

Yet beneath the stillness, a pulse of wisdom beats. The same intuition that once kept her ancestors alive now calls her to evolve. When Stella begins to recognize the inherited stories, 'money is hard,' 'men can't be trusted,' 'I must do everything myself,' they start to loosen their grip. Awareness becomes her first act of rebellion.

Healing for Stella doesn't mean rejecting her past; it means rewriting her role in it. She honors her lineage by transforming its energy. She learns that her ancestors didn't endure so she could stay stuck. They endured so she could *be free.*

In every Stagnant Stella lies a cycle-breaker in waiting, a woman learning that stillness is not stagnation but the sacred pause before movement. When she finally exhales the old narratives and chooses a new rhythm, she becomes the bridge between what was and what will be.

She fears the unknown, and every sound, rustle, or movement makes her more afraid to move forward. I had a client we'll call Zahra, who came to me looking for answers and inspiration. She knew something was wrong but didn't know how to feel better. Zahra attended one of my retreats after participating in an online wellness session I did for her job. The mindfulness work I shared with the participants really spoke to her, and she joined my email list. As soon as I announced my yoga retreat, she paid in full!

Zahra's life was changing, and everything in her wanted to grab ahold of a lifeline because she felt as if she was drowning. Ahead was retirement after 30 years, a daughter in college after graduating during the Covid-19 pandemic, and an older daughter coming out of an extremely abusive relationship with a young child.

When she booked three months of one-on-one coaching with me, she was on the verge of divorce and felt more lost than ever. Zahra told me she was depressed and had difficulty getting out of bed, let alone getting dressed.

Stagnant Stellas are dedicated workers. They tend to work for an organization or corporation for decades. They become experts in their fields but don't realize they could soar in their zone of genius. They don't cause many waves or disturbances at work but stay because they have been there for years. When they retire, they tend to feel lost, directionless.

Zahra wanted peace but contributed to the chaos in her family's life. She needed stability, but she doubted her decisions and second guessed her choices. She wished for control but kept losing herself in her own confusion.

The Cycle She Was Born Into

What Zahra eventually came to understand was that her struggle didn't begin with her. Her patterns of silence and self-protection mirrored the same survival strategies she'd witnessed in her family. Her mother's harshness hadn't been cruelty alone. It was armor, shaped by her own unhealed pain. When Zahra tried to tell someone about the abuse she endured as a child and wasn't believed, she learned that her voice was dangerous, that truth came with punishment or disbelief. So she buried her words deep inside herself, vowing never to make waves again.

Decades later, that same silencing reappeared as hesitation, overthinking, and emotional outbursts. Every time she swallowed her feelings to keep the peace or doubted her instincts to avoid conflict, she was unconsciously reenacting her mother's story. The fear of being dismissed had become the filter through which she lived her adult life.

During our coaching, we began using the Feelings Wheel to locate where her words had been stuck. Each emotion she named, whether hurt, betrayed, or unseen, became a key unlocking years of suppressed truth. It wasn't easy. Naming her feelings felt like learning a forgotten language. But as she gave voice to what had once been silenced, she saw how every unspoken word had tethered her to the past.

That realization was the turning point. Zahra recognized that the little girl who couldn't speak had become the woman who couldn't ask for help. The cycle was never about weakness; it was about survival. And now that she could see it, she could choose differently.

For the first time, she understood that awareness itself was freedom. Her voice, shaky, tender, new, became the beginning of her awakening.

Her struggles were with self-confidence, inner peace, acceptance, and belief in herself. She hated her life and was dissatisfied with her choices. Because a Stella wanted to make her family proud of her and to keep the peace, she sacrificed her dreams. Now that she is older, her bottled-up emotions are getting the best of her. They cloud her judgment, skew her decisions, and negatively impact her relationship with family and friends. She lashes out at and argues with the people who are closest to her. Stella cries almost every day because she doesn't know how to change things and is on the verge of giving up.

Her brain is like a reptile: unevolved and focused on food, shelter, and safety. She goes to work, pays her bills, does her best to keep the home clean, and starts all over again the next day. She is stuck in a rut, fearing change and risks. The world seems threatening, and people are untrustworthy. All this leads to emotional outbursts, difficulty focusing, and a general feeling of being on edge.

Stella does have aspirations and dreams, but fear and self-doubt keep her paralyzed. The "what ifs" keep her from pursuing her passions, leaving her feeling stuck and frustrated. Most of her conversations are on a loop of the same topics or stuck on "woulda, coulda, shoulda."

I have a feeling you're thinking Stagnant Stella is a lost cause. She's not. There is hope. She needs to be willing to take a step toward the light of freedom. Stella must decide to change. She must decide to do something different and new. She must decide that she no longer wants to live how she has been for so long. When she does, she is beginning the journey of Awakening.

Awakening is the willingness to see, feel, and know that your life isn't working. It is the maturity of accepting responsibility for your choices without blame or shame. It is the removal of guilt, people-pleasing, and excuses. Awakening is acceptance, excitement, and a new mindset.

Zahra's story is a mirror for countless Stagnant Stellas: women who aren't broken, but burdened by inherited survival patterns.

THE THREE ARCHETYPES

Which one are you right now?

STAGNANT STELLA

She sees what needs to change but can't seem to move.

- Feels stuck in patterns she can't explain
- Waits for life to change on its own
- Knows something is wrong but can't name it
- Struggles to make decisions and follow through
- Lives in survival mode without realizing it

SEARCHING SERENA

She's doing all the work but still feels lost.

- Reads every book, attends every workshop
- Makes progress then slides back
- Knows the words but can't embody them
- Works hard but spins in circles
- Searching for the missing piece

THRIVING THERESA

She has done the work. Now she lives it.

- Rooted in her identity and values
- Makes aligned decisions with confidence
- Feels happy, whole, and free
- Her healing has shifted her entire family
- She is a Luxenary of her own becoming

Every Theresa was once a Stella.

The Awakened Woman Archetypes

When the Whisper Gets Too Loud to Ignore

Awakening rarely arrives with fireworks. It begins quietly, with a pattern you can't ignore anymore. A repeated argument. A familiar heartbreak. A moment when you hear yourself say, *"How did I get here again?"*

For Stagnant Stella, and for women like Zahra, that awakening begins with a whisper of recognition. The moment you realize your choices have been shaped more by fear than freedom. The moment you understand your story doesn't have to mirror your family's.

For years, Zahra believed endurance was strength. Her mother had survived by pushing through pain, and she learned to do the same. But strength without softness hardens into self-protection, and protection without expression becomes isolation. Zahra began to see that what she once called "being responsible" was really being afraid to dream. Her awakening began the moment she could name that truth.

Pattern recognition is sacred work. It requires humility and courage to look at the cycles we've normalized: staying in jobs that drain us, maintaining relationships out of guilt, replaying emotional scripts that no longer serve us. Most of these patterns aren't personal flaws; they're inherited defense mechanisms. Awakening happens when we stop asking, *"What's wrong with me?"* and start asking, *"What am I repeating, and why?"*

For many women, this recognition feels like both relief and grief. Relief because we finally understand we're not broken. Grief because we see how much of our lives were spent living someone else's survival story. But awareness is the doorway to liberation. Once we see the pattern, we can choose something new.

Awakening is not an event; it's a threshold. It's the moment you realize that peace, joy, and purpose are not luxuries for other people. They are birthrights that require intention. Awakening calls you to step out of autopilot and into authorship.

When Zahra began to name her emotions, she discovered that awareness without action creates tension. The soul wants movement once it sees truth. Her next step was to explore what she truly wanted, beyond obligation, beyond fear. That curiosity marked the shift from stagnation to seeking.

That's where **Searching Serena** enters the story. Serena hears the same whisper Stella did, but she chooses to follow it. She begins her quest for clarity, identity, and freedom, not because everything is falling apart, but because she finally believes something more is possible.

Awakening is the moment the light comes on. Seeking is what happens when you decide to walk toward it.

Working with clients like Zahra taught me something unexpected: awakening follows predictable patterns, patterns that transcend individual stories and reveal the universal cycles of transformation woven through every family line.

Luxe Lifestyle Ritual: The 5-Minute Awakening Check-In

This ritual helps Stagnant Stellas notice the moment they shift from autopilot into awakening.

Step 1: Name the Pattern

- Ask yourself: "What am I repeating that no longer feels aligned?"

Step 2: Name the Feeling

- Use the Feelings Wheel or a simple sentence like: "Right now I feel ___ because ___."

Step 3: Choose a Micro-Movement

- One tiny step: a text drafted, a boundary whispered, a small pause before reacting.

Step 4: Affirm Your Agency

- Say: "I am allowed to choose differently now."

Step 5: Close With Stillness

- 30 seconds of silence. Let the nervous system feel the shift.

This ritual is gentle, doable, and honors the chapter's theme that awakening begins quietly.

LUXENARY BRIDGE: Your Next Evolution

Stagnant Stella is the woman who feels the weight of inherited hesitation: the pause, the freeze, the overwhelm that comes from carrying generations of uncertainty. It's the soul saying, "There is more for you than this."

Your awareness of being stuck means you're already shifting.

In the next chapter, you'll meet **Searching Serena**. The woman who begins to question, explore, and awaken. She is the first spark of movement in a family line that may have been still for decades. She doesn't have all the answers, but she has the courage to start seeking them.

She is your next evolution. The version of you who chooses curiosity over complacency, possibility over paralysis, and alignment over autopilot.

You're not waking up; you're rising.

REFLECTION PROMPTS (Stagnant Stella)

Use these prompts to deepen your awareness of where you're stuck and where you're ready to shift:

1. What family patterns do you recognize showing up in your life right now?

2. Where are you waiting instead of acting, repeating the hesitation of previous generations?

3. What dreams have you quietly talked yourself out of because you didn't feel ready, worthy, or supported?

4. How do you tend to respond when you feel overwhelmed: freeze, retreat, procrastinate, or shut down?

5. Where in your life are you hoping things will "magically get better" without any real change?

6. What would breaking your family's cycles look like for you: practically, emotionally, spiritually?

7. When was the last time you felt truly excited about your future, independent of anyone else's expectations?

8. What is one small decision you've been postponing that could begin your shift from stagnation to movement this week?

DAWNISM

"Stagnation is not failure. It's feedback."

AFFIRMATIONS

I am willing to see my patterns with honesty and compassion. I release the belief that I must shrink to stay safe. My awareness is the first step toward my freedom. I choose movement over stagnation and truth over silence.

Chapter 4
YOU'VE READ EVERY BOOK. WHY ARE YOU STILL HERE?

Searching Serena and the moment she realizes more information isn't the answer

Have you ever felt like you're constantly searching for more but unsure where to start? That was me after recognizing I didn't want to repeat my mother's story.

I was awakening to patterns and cycles of generational patterns and sadness. When I started checking off my list of 42 things for my 42nd year, I knew I never wanted to go through that way of life again.

In 2012, I read a book by Rick Warren, *The Purpose Driven Life*, and decided to create a new legacy for my children based on his teachings. I wrote a letter about my past struggles for my children and my stepbrother's daughter, my niece. They were all on the verge of making big life decisions such as motherhood, college selection, and career choices. I started to believe the time for keeping secrets was over.

I had always felt that if I knew more about my mother's struggles, I might not have repeated them. The book encouraged this practice. I wanted to remove the veil from my life for the children I influenced. I remember my son having a hard time finding out some of the things I went through and decisions I made, but now he knew. The truth was on the table. And telling the truth is often the first step to breaking a cycle.

The Difference Between Searching and Seeking

There's a difference between searching and seeking.

Searching often comes from fear, from the part of us that's desperate to fill a void, to fix what feels broken, or to find the missing piece we believe will make us whole. It's grasping for answers outside of ourselves. Searching says, "Something is wrong with me, and I need to find what's missing."

Seeking, on the other hand, comes from curiosity and trust. It's an inward journey, a soft but determined return to your own truth. Seeking says, "The answers are already within me. I'm just remembering."

Many women spend years searching for validation, for love, for peace. What they're really longing for is alignment.

The shift happens the moment you stop searching for what's missing and start seeking what's real. That's when healing begins.

The Day I Understood Why I Chose My Mother

I once asked my Reiki master, Annette, a question that had haunted me for years:

"Why did I have to have a mother who was depressed, unsupportive, and dissatisfied with life?"

Annette smiled softly and said, "You picked your mom."

I think I yelled, "WHAT? Why would I ever do that?"

She looked at me with so much compassion and said, "To end the cycle."

I cried for the rest of that session.

Reiki, a Japanese energy-healing practice, has often reminded me of the "laying on of hands" I witnessed in church as a teenager. It's a channeling of unconditional love through an attuned practitioner, directed to the parts of the body and soul that are asking to be healed. But that day, the healing was energetic and ancestral.

For the first time, I began to understand that maybe my mother's pain was the classroom where I learned compassion, boundaries, and purpose. Maybe her silence was the echo that taught me how to find my own voice.

I didn't choose her story; I chose to transform it.

Why Some Women Become the Cycle-Breakers

Some women are born to continue the story. Others are called to rewrite it.

Cycle-breakers are those who hear the quiet whisper that says, "It ends with me." They don't choose the easiest path. They choose the one that heals generations. The work is rarely glamorous. It looks like crying in therapy instead of pretending everything's fine. It feels like setting boundaries that disappoint people you love. It sounds like forgiveness, not because they deserve it, but because you do.

Cycle-breaking isn't about blame. It's about awareness. It's about choosing to rise above inherited pain and rewrite the emotional DNA of your lineage.

That's what Searching Serena represents: the woman who feels the restlessness, hears the whisper, and starts looking for another way.

THE THREE ARCHETYPES

Which one are you right now?

STAGNANT STELLA

She sees what needs to change but can't seem to move.

- Feels stuck in patterns she can't explain
- Waits for life to change on its own
- Knows something is wrong but can't name it
- Struggles to make decisions and follow through
- Lives in survival mode without realizing it

SEARCHING SERENA

She's doing all the work but still feels lost.

- Reads every book, attends every workshop
- Makes progress then slides back
- Knows the words but can't embody them
- Works hard but spins in circles
- Searching for the missing piece

THRIVING THERESA

She has done the work. Now she lives it.

- Rooted in her identity and values
- Makes aligned decisions with confidence
- Feels happy, whole, and free
- Her healing has shifted her entire family
- She is a Luxenary of her own becoming

Every Theresa was once a Stella.

The Awakened Woman Archetypes

CELESTE: THE WOMAN WHO KEPT GOING BACK

Searching Serenas are my most common archetype. As I've worked with yoga students and teachers, as well as coaching clients over the years, this is the type of woman I attract the most to my work.

Meet Celeste. She was someone I knew from my days as a school librarian. When she was in high school, Celeste had trouble finding her way. She played sports and was looking for a way to connect with others. At the time she was also struggling with her sexuality and sexual identity. There were disagreements with her parents, and she turned to promiscuous behavior when she felt rejected. She ended up dropping out of high school when she became pregnant.

Many years later, I saw a Facebook post where she was asking for recommendations for a life coach. She had moved thousands of miles away, raised her son, earned her GED, and was working a decent-paying job. However, she was divorcing and felt once again that her life choices had stalled her progress.

Celeste second-guessed her decisions. She was haunted by her wife's hurtful words and was searching for a more peaceful and fulfilling life. She had made strides but kept going back to her old habits and familiar patterns. The people she kept attracting into her life had similar abusive tendencies. They belittled and put her down. These folks were holding her back from being great.

Typical story, right? Once you decide to make changes in your life, those who like you under their control often get upset.

Searching Serenas are amazing because they are constantly seeking self-improvement. But remember, progress takes time.

Finding consistency can be a struggle, especially when self-doubt creeps in.

When Celeste and I started working together, she lacked direction and wanted to do everything at once. She said she wanted to lose weight, work out every day, make more money, move to another state, repair her relationship with her mother, and on and on.

Searching Serenas are ready to take action; however, they lack foresight and proper planning. They tend to be impulsive and impatient. They have tons of ideas and get frustrated when things don't work out as planned.

However, Searching Serenas know it's time for a change. They have a burning passion to have a better life. This is why they tend to be high-achieving people who keep wanting to improve themselves.

Searching Serena might be a teacher working on her PhD who wants to be a consultant, while doing standup comedy gigs with a t-shirt line and running for city council. These are real people, y'all. I've had discovery calls with them, and they shared these big plans of theirs with me.

The point is these women are searching. Most of the time, they have low self-esteem and are filling their lives with awards, accolades, and accomplishments to try to make themselves feel worthy. They often have a hard time being still and focusing on one thing at a time.

Please know that she has great potential and is capable of achieving almost anything she puts her mind to. Searching Serenas are highly coachable and responsive to feedback. She wants a life that is different, better, and new.

This was Celeste. She had come so far in her self-development. I reminded her to pause and look at all she had done. Like most Searching Serenas, Celeste kept looking at how far she wanted to go, not how far she had come.

When She Stopped Fighting the Mirror

As we talked, Celeste began to see how the chaos in her adult life mirrored the pain she'd absorbed as a child. Her mother's ridicule had shaped her inner critic, and the rejection she felt as a teenager had turned into a pattern of seeking love through struggle. What she thought were "bad choices" were really old coping mechanisms, inherited scripts that said, *You'll only be loved if you fight for it.*

That awareness was powerful. Celeste realized that her mother's harshness wasn't personal. It was the only language of survival she had learned. The difference was that Celeste was ready to learn a new one. Through our work together, she practiced using words her family had never used openly, words like peace, boundaries, forgiveness, and joy.

Each time she chose calm over conflict and communication over chaos, she was rewriting her family's story. Breaking generational patterns isn't loud or glamorous.

It's often quiet work: sending a text instead of starting a fight, saying "no" without guilt, resting without apology. Every small act of self-honoring was a declaration: *It stops with me.*

We worked on one task at a time, celebrated her consistency, and then moved on to the next area. We began by creating a framework with a theme. The framework would be used to help her manage decisions, relationships, and career goals. She identified her core values, designed her personal mission statement, and expanded her vision. Celeste came to every session excited and motivated. Once she let go of the need to fix it all at once, she set herself free to thrive.

Celeste tapped into a tunnel-vision focus mode. She gave herself grace and focused on one small, consistent step forward at a time. Her ex-wife told her she wasn't consistent, but I pointed out how she had set a goal to move out of her small Midwestern town and go out west with little support or community, and she did it. She found a job, began to excel at it, and was asked to move into leadership roles. Her emotional intelligence had taken a beating, and she second-guessed her own feelings, but her actions were telling a very different story.

We also used one of my favorite coaching tools, the Feelings Wheel, to help Celeste put words to emotions she'd spent a lifetime suppressing. Most women of color were taught to be seen and not heard. They were told the way they felt wasn't true or valid. For example, when little Black girls would get their hair braided and cry out in pain or discomfort, they were told to be quiet or labeled as tender-headed. Over time, these girls learned to suppress or numb their feelings.

Using the Feelings Wheel to pinpoint how we truly feel is powerful. In my experience, when we use words with a deeper level of meaning, it helps others understand where we are and what we need from them.

Words have power and they become things.

The Feelings Wheel starts with surface or primary emotions. Then the next ring is a higher level or secondary set of feelings. Then it culminates and broadens in the final ring or tertiary level.

For Celeste, using the Feelings Wheel became more than an exercise in emotional intelligence; it was a bridge back to her voice. Each word she named rewrote a story she had inherited from generations of women who were told to be quiet, to endure, to stay small. She realized that the same silence that had protected her mother now imprisoned her. By naming her feelings out loud, Celeste wasn't describing emotions. She was reclaiming agency. Her framework became the structure her lineage never had, a safe container for clarity, boundaries, and self-trust.

Through that framework, she began to make decisions rooted not in fear, but in alignment. Each step forward, no matter how small, became an act of defiance against the belief that she was destined to repeat her past. Celeste's work was not about fixing her life overnight; it was about taking ownership of it, one truth at a time.

That's how Searching Serenas evolve, through conscious pattern interruption. They shift from victims of their circumstances to creators of their destiny. The framework they build becomes both map and mirror, a reminder that structure isn't control. It's freedom. And when a woman learns to turn awareness into a system of self-leadership, she doesn't change her own life. She changes her lineage.

If you see yourself in Celeste, here's how we begin this work together:

- Start small. Break down your goals into smaller, achievable steps. This makes them feel less overwhelming and allows you to celebrate progress along the way.

- Then find an accountability partner. Share your goals with a friend, family member, or coach who can support and motivate you. You don't have to walk this path alone.

Searching Serena: The Designated Healer

Searching Serena is starting to explore self-improvement but faces challenges. She might dip her toes into the self-care waters but struggles with consistency. She knows there is a need for change but isn't sure how to implement it fully.

Searching Serena represents a woman in the early stages of transformation. She's seeking answers and making efforts, but she needs guidance and support.

Every family has one. The woman who feels everything a little deeper, who asks the hard questions, who can't ignore the tension everyone else sweeps under the rug. She's the empath, the truth-teller, the emotional first responder. Searching Serena didn't apply for this role. She was initiated into it by circumstance and soul contract.

She is the "designated healer."

Not because she has all the answers, but because she can no longer pretend the wounds aren't there. Her sensitivity is both her compass and her curriculum. She absorbs the energy in the room, senses the unspoken pain, and instinctively tries to soothe it. It's exhausting at times, carrying what isn't hers, but it's also sacred.

When Serena learns that she's not responsible for her family's healing but called to model what healing looks like, everything changes. Her role shifts from fixer to way-shower. She becomes the living permission slip for everyone else to rise.

The Burden and Gift of Being the One Who Seeks Change

Searching Serena carries a paradox in her heart. The ache for more and the guilt for wanting it. Change can feel like betrayal when loyalty has been her love language. She looks around and wonders, *Why can't I be content like everyone else?*

But the desire for more isn't greed. It's guidance. It's her soul whispering, *There's another way.* The burden is that she feels the gap between who she is and who she's meant to be. The gift is that she's brave enough to cross it.

Seeking change often means disappointing the status quo. It means being misunderstood, even resented, by those who fear transformation. Yet the same courage that isolates her at first will one day inspire the very people who doubted her. That's the alchemy of a cycle-breaker; turning pain into purpose and rebellion into renewal.

Magnetic but Scattered: The Serena Paradox

Searching Serena is magnetic because she's in motion. The universe loves momentum. Her curiosity, openness, and hunger for growth act like a beacon, drawing in teachers, invitations, and synchronicities. She's the woman who "just happens" to meet the right person, stumble upon the perfect course, or receive the unexpected offer.

But abundance without alignment can become noise. The more she evolves, the more Serena must practice discernment. She has to ask, *Does this opportunity feed my expansion or my ego?*

When she learns to focus her energy, opportunities stop feeling like detours and start feeling like destiny. Her power lies not in doing more, but in choosing what's meant.

A mantra for her chapter might be: **"I no longer chase every open door. I trust the one that feels like home."**

How I Found My Way Back to Myself in a Parking Lot

It began with what seemed like an ordinary inconvenience, a head cold that turned into a full sinus infection. I had pushed through for days until I finally booked a pharmacy appointment, hoping for relief. But I went to the wrong location, was late getting to the correct one, and when I asked for help, the nurses dismissed me without a glance. No one else was waiting. They simply refused to see me.

I left angry, tired, and sick, but the illness wasn't totally physical. It was layered with something older, decades of being unheard, unseen, and unconsidered. I sat in the car, tears streaming, and somewhere between exhaustion and surrender, a quiet thought surfaced: *Use your words.*

So I did. I called my insurance company and, instead of complaining, I named what was actually happening inside me. The representative asked me how I was doing, and I told her the truth.

"I feel depleted, defeated, discouraged, drained, distraught, demeaned, disregarded, and disrespected."

The representative paused, then said softly, "I'm so sorry you've been treated this way. Let me help you right now." Within minutes she had arranged an appointment and resolved everything.

That was the day I realized that language, especially emotional language, is medicine.

I grew up in a generation, and in a culture, where emotional expression was often considered indulgent or unsafe. Many women of color were taught to be seen and not heard. Strength meant silence; survival meant suppression. Feelings were luxuries we couldn't afford.

But silence becomes heavy. Unspoken emotions don't disappear; they lodge themselves in the body, manifesting as tension, fatigue, even illness. The moment I articulated my feelings, my body began to release what it had been holding.

During the pandemic, I connected with a therapist friend through Tara Pringle Jefferson's group, The Self Care Suite. She introduced me to a visual called The Feelings Wheel. I remember staring at it as if I were decoding a map back to myself. At the center were the primary emotions: sad, angry, fearful. Around them spiraled the deeper layers: loneliness, rejection, shame, grief, powerlessness. For the first time, I could see the complexity of what I had simplified or denied.

I began using the wheel as an intentional practice. Instead of saying "I'm fine," I tried on more precise language:

I feel unseen.
I feel hopeful.
I feel hesitant but willing.

Each word pulled another thread of awareness through my life.

Precision became power. The clearer I became about what I was feeling, the faster clarity followed, in my body, in my choices, in my relationships. I stopped fighting to be understood and started understanding myself.

When I later introduced the Feelings Wheel to clients, I saw the same awakening. They would trace their finger across its circles and whisper, "I didn't even know I could feel all of this." That's when I recognized this wasn't only a therapeutic tool. It was a portal. It opened the door to the frameworks I've created since, my first signature system before I had language for systems at all.

Looking back, that day in the car was the beginning of The Luxe Identity Spiral™. Awareness had found me in a parking lot, wrapped in tissues and tears. By naming my feelings, I accessed the first Spiral Point: emotion, awareness, and action in alignment.

Every evolution I've made since, every lesson on self-leadership, boundaries, and sovereignty, began with that simple but radical act of telling the truth about how I felt.

The Feelings Wheel became my first true tool of transformation. It wasn't only a chart of emotions. It was a framework for awareness, the seed that grew into what I now teach about alignment, embodiment, and freedom. What began as a moment of frustration in a car turned into the foundation of my life's work.

So when I think of tools, this is where I begin: the Feelings Wheel. Not as a chart on a wall, but as a compass that returns me, again and again, to the center of myself.

What Celeste Sparked in Me

Watching Celeste create her personal framework based on the techniques I teach lit something up in me. I had already built my own path out of generational pain, but seeing her take ownership of her life in such a structured way made me realize something important, patterns can be interrupted on purpose.

Celeste wasn't "just doing better." She was following a map. Her values, mission, and vision became her internal GPS. When old habits tried to pull her back, she had something to return to, a written, living reminder of who she was becoming.

I started to notice the same thing with other Searching Serenas. Once we identified a theme for their season, clarified their values, and created a simple framework for decision-making, everything shifted. It wasn't perfect or linear, but it was intentional. They weren't wholly reacting to life anymore. They were responding with clarity.

That's when a deeper question rose up in me:

What if frameworks weren't exclusively helpful for a few clients? What if there was a complete system for breaking generational patterns? What if transformation could be systematized and taught?

I realized that my years of teaching yoga, my Path to the Awakened Woman framework, and the tools like the Feelings Wheel weren't random. They were pieces of a larger pattern. Every time a woman like Celeste stopped searching from fear and started seeking from alignment, the same elements kept showing up: awareness, language, boundaries, structure, support, and a willingness to choose a different story.

The more I paid attention, the clearer it became. This wasn't solely about my story or Celeste's story. There was a spiral of transformation repeating itself across different women, different ages, different backgrounds.

The librarian in me wanted to catalog it. The coach in me wanted to teach it. The cycle-breaker in me wanted to share it with as many women as possible.

Celeste's framework was the spark. The Luxe Identity Spiral™ was the fire.

Before a Searching Serena can step into her next identity, she has to face the first and most uncomfortable part of evolution: truth. Awareness shows you the pattern, but integrity breaks it. Celeste learned that clarity means nothing without boundaries, and emotional insight means little without honest self-leadership. Every Seeking Woman eventually arrives at the same question: *Now that I know better, how do I live better?*

That's the turning point.

Awareness is like turning on a light in a long-dark room. **Integrity is choosing to clean what you now see.**

This is where Searching Serena begins to rise from seeking to becoming, from understanding her patterns to rewriting them.

LUXENARY BRIDGE: Your Next Evolution

Your transition into the next spiral point

Searching Serena is the woman who begins to question, explore, and awaken. She's the designated healer, the pattern-spotter, the one who dares to look at what everyone else avoids. But seeking is only the beginning. There is a deeper evolution waiting. The woman who doesn't singularly search for her potential, she lives it boldly and out loud.

In the next chapter, you'll meet **Thriving Theresa**: the version of you who has crossed the threshold, claimed her power, and begun to embody the life she once only imagined.

REFLECTION PROMPTS (Searching Serena)

Use these prompts to deepen your Searching Serena awakening:

1. Where do you still search for validation outside of yourself?

2. What are you seeking that your mother, grandmother, or lineage never had permission to desire?

3. Which patterns in your life feel like echoes of childhood coping mechanisms?

4. Where do you confuse movement with progress?

5. What emotions arise when you slow down enough to feel instead of fix?

6. Which opportunities feel aligned and which ones feel like distractions?

7. What does "seeking from truth instead of fear" look like for you?

8. What is one small, consistent action that could help you break a lifelong pattern this month?

DAWNISM

"You're not confused. You're awakening."

AFFIRMATIONS

I honor the woman I'm becoming. I release the fear that kept me searching outside myself. I trust the answers already rising within me. I take one aligned step at a time, with clarity and courage. I am capable, I am worthy, and I am ready for more.

Chapter 5
THE WOMAN SHE PRAYED YOU'D BECOME

Thriving Theresa and the moment she becomes who she needed

I recently heard on a podcast someone say that for Black people, "the past is painful, the present is precarious, but the future is free." Our ancestors lived out of the idea of 'one day.' They held on to the hope that you and I would get here. As you heal, reprogram, and sever the bonds that kept us from that freedom they dreamed of and hoped for, you will be creating a future not only for yourself but for your descendants.

Imagine being the ancestor your descendants thank for creating a legacy of happy, whole, and abundant lives.

Thriving Theresa is the woman who has stood in the gap between the past and the present. She has learned that her life is her own. Mentoring younger women is a pleasure and a privilege for her. Her participation in programs and activities is a balance of paid and volunteer opportunities. She knows the value of her work and worth, so when she charges her rate, she is demonstrating to others how it should be done. Thriving Theresa lives joyously and has built in practices that keep her nervous system regulated and at peace. She believes in balance because nature has proven its possible. When she interacts with her family, she knows their stories are not hers. Their patterns don't have to inform or influence her life. She respectfully and with honor shares her own experiences with them to be an example of change.

Being a cycle-breaker is a responsibility and privilege for Thriving Theresa. She decided when she raised her children things would be different. She would parent with kindness, structure, and support. Her children could be seen and heard. Other Thriving Theresas consciously decided to not have children. She felt her gifts were better used through other avenues such as mentoring, speaking, teaching, leading and sharing. Some are aunts, godmothers, or "big sisters" and this fills her cup and theirs. Her main tool is using boundaries to keep herself from over-giving or taking on too much responsibility. Her family, friends, and organizations know this and respect her even more because of it.

She Didn't Get Lucky. She Got Intentional.

Thriving Theresa is the woman who stands in the sacred space between what was and what can be. She is the bridge, the builder, and the blueprint for a new legacy. Her journey is not about striving for more but *living* from a place of wholeness. After years of healing, learning, and unlearning, she has found her rhythm, a life designed with intention, balance, and peace.

For Theresa, thriving doesn't mean constant motion. It means alignment. It means waking up with clarity, leading with grace, and allowing her energy to flow where it's most impactful. She has learned that freedom isn't found in achievement alone but in the ability to choose how she spends her time, shares her gifts, and protects her peace.

She has done the hard inner work, examining her family patterns, naming the inherited beliefs that once held her hostage, and choosing to evolve instead of repeat. Her journey is defined by awareness and action. She recognizes that breaking cycles is both a responsibility and a privilege. She no longer carries her family's emotional or financial struggles as her own. Instead, she uses her growth as a model of what's possible.

Theresa creates new generational patterns through her daily choices. She speaks truthfully even when it's uncomfortable. She rests without guilt. She earns and spends money consciously, creating wealth that feels ethical and expansive. She sets boundaries with love, refusing to over-give as a way to prove worth. Every act of alignment becomes a lesson for those watching her: her children, nieces, mentees, or peers.

But being *different* from your family isn't easy. Theresa has learned that growth often feels like betrayal to those who are still surviving. Her evolution has been met with both admiration and misunderstanding. Some family members call her "lucky" or "bougie," not realizing her life is built on daily discipline and self-awareness. Others still expect her to rescue, fix, or carry emotional weight that isn't hers.

Instead of shrinking to make others comfortable, she has learned to stay grounded in compassion. She honors her family without repeating their patterns. She visits but doesn't move back in energetically. She gives from overflow, not obligation. She practices gratitude for the sacrifices that made her freedom possible, while refusing to let guilt dictate her growth.

Theresa also understands that consistency is her evolution's classroom. Even after years of healing, there are days when she slips into old rhythms: working too long, saying yes too quickly, or doubting her timing. But now, she notices faster. She uses those moments not as proof of failure but as reminders of progress. Her awareness turns every relapse into revelation.

The biggest shift is that Theresa no longer defines thriving by perfection. She defines it by peace. She knows that discipline doesn't restrict her. It refines her. Structure gives her space. Ritual gives her rhythm. Through it all, she embodies what legacy truly means, not only what you leave behind, but what you live now.

She is the ancestor her descendants will thank. Not because she did everything flawlessly, but because she modeled what healing, self-trust, and sacred boundaries look like in real time.

THE THREE ARCHETYPES

Which one are you right now?

STAGNANT STELLA

She sees what needs to change but can't seem to move.

- Feels stuck in patterns she can't explain
- Waits for life to change on its own
- Knows something is wrong but can't name it
- Struggles to make decisions and follow through
- Lives in survival mode without realizing it

SEARCHING SERENA

She's doing all the work but still feels lost.

- Reads every book, attends every workshop
- Makes progress then slides back
- Knows the words but can't embody them
- Works hard but spins in circles
- Searching for the missing piece

THRIVING THERESA

She has done the work. Now she lives it.

- Rooted in her identity and values
- Makes aligned decisions with confidence
- Feels happy, whole, and free
- Her healing has shifted her entire family
- She is a Luxenary of her own becoming

Every Theresa was once a Stella.

The Awakened Woman Archetypes

DARA: THE FIRST WOMAN IN HER LINE TO CHOOSE HER WHOLE SELF

Before: The Life That Looked Full but Wasn't

When Dara first walked into the back room of that martial arts dojo where I was holding the earliest version of Daybreak Yoga, she was already what many would call successful. She held leadership roles in higher education, was deeply involved in her church, volunteered regularly, and prioritized her health. From the outside, her life looked full.

But as she later shared with me, "I had a professional career. I had leadership roles. But I still desired more. I needed to understand Dara."

Despite all her accomplishments, something inside felt incomplete. "I needed space," she said, "space to come back to myself."

This is the quiet truth of so many high-achieving women, especially Black women conditioned to serve, perform, and persevere. The world applauded Dara's productivity, but her spirit was tired. She had spent decades giving to everyone except herself.

Her introduction to yoga began in the 1990s at a gym, but when she found Daybreak Yoga, everything changed. "It was the community, the energy, the people," she said. "It invited me to understand yoga as a way of life, not just exercise."

The PhD That Went Uncelebrated

At our first retreat in an Ohio national park, a conversation about celebration revealed something pivotal. Dara quietly admitted she had earned her PhD but had never celebrated it.

Her reasoning was steeped in generational humility: "By telling everyone I had accomplished such a milestone, that was being boastful. How dare you think of yourself as being great."

Her parents hadn't finished high school. She grew up in the projects where people doubted she'd make it to college, let alone a doctorate. Yet even after defying every statistic, she couldn't own her success.

That retreat changed everything. We celebrated her. We affirmed her. Something shifted. "It was liberating," she said. "I felt like I could walk in purpose. I was no longer holding on to this little package. I could finally focus on what comes next."

For Dara, that moment of celebration was more than acknowledgement. It was an ancestral release. She stopped apologizing for her brilliance and began moving through the world with permission to shine.

During: When the Mat Became the Mirror

Dara didn't stop there. She kept saying yes: to retreats, to teacher training, to The Business of Yoga Academy. "It allowed me to go in, in order to show out," she said. "You gotta start in."

Through this process, Dara restructured her life. She learned to say no without guilt, to extend herself grace, and to trust her timing. She confronted fear through crow pose, a balancing posture that terrified her until she finally lifted her feet and shouted, "Did you see that?"

Each practice became a metaphor. "People think I'm just doing this pose," she said. "No, no, no. The mat is life."

She launched her consulting company, applying what she learned about abundance, systems, and overflow. When friends questioned her for hiring help, she laughed. "Because I live in overflow. A person in overflow would never question that."

After: The Woman Who Gave Herself Permission

Dara continued to rise, from professor to vice provost to consultant. She discovered financial freedom and emotional peace. Her decisions became guided by alignment, not fear. "My planner told me, 'Girl, you can do anything you want,'" she recalled. "That's when I realized I had been living in survival mode out of habit, not necessity."

At home, she created rituals of peace: yoga mats in every room, a meditation corner, recited affirmations, money pinned throughout her house. When emotion rises, she turns to her mat, breath, and movement to release it.

Her influence extends far beyond herself. By embodying peace, she became the example. Her nieces see that security doesn't require self-sacrifice. Her colleagues now ask her to lead breathing practices in meetings. She mentors young women, reminding them, "Don't die on every hill. You're here to win the war of becoming yourself."

When her brother passed, Dara recognized his newborn grandson, born almost to the date of his death, as divine continuation. Legacy in motion.

THE INHERITED BLUEPRINT: The First Woman in the Line to Choose Her Whole Self

Dara often quotes Marianne Williamson: *"As we let our own light shine, we unconsciously give others permission to do the same."*

Her transformation became an energetic inheritance. She healed forward, proving that thriving is not perfection: it's integration. As she put it, "You're thriving, but you're gonna get a scar here, you're gonna trip over that. It's about the growth, the experience."

Dara is the living embodiment of Thriving Theresa: the woman who broke cycles, built systems, and made healing her family's new tradition. She is the ancestor her descendants will thank.

The System Beneath the Spiral

Understanding your archetype is the beginning. Awareness awakens the woman, but structure sustains her. Once I understood my own archetype, I realized awareness wasn't the finish line. It was the first gate. Healing without structure is temporary. Growth without rhythm eventually unravels. The real work wasn't merely in awakening; it was in organizing the awakening.

What happens after you recognize your patterns? How do you hold your expansion when the inspiration fades? Awareness opens the door. Systemization keeps it open. That's where transformation shifts from personal insight to lasting embodiment.

I began to notice a pattern among the women I worked with: smart, self-aware, deeply committed to growth. They journaled, meditated, and did the inner work, yet they kept circling the same lessons. They knew what to do, but not how to sustain it. Breakthroughs faded because there was no structure to hold them.

I saw brilliant women leave retreats feeling unstoppable, only to fall back into burnout weeks later. Not because they lacked willpower, but because they didn't have a system to support their expansion once daily life returned. They were transforming in spirit but collapsing in structure. Healing needs scaffolding. Without a framework, inspiration drifts away. What we needed was something cyclical, something that honored growth as a living process rather than a one-time revelation.

When I started mapping the transformation process I witnessed in myself and my clients, I realized every woman's growth followed a rhythm. It wasn't random. It was a repeatable pattern. Awareness was always the first step. It lit the match. Then came affirmation, the rebuilding of belief and self-worth. Finally came aligned action, the integration of new behavior that created tangible change.

I began to see that transformation wasn't linear. **It was cyclical.** Each new level of growth required returning to the same three steps with deeper understanding. It wasn't about hustling harder or reaching higher. It was about spiraling inward, refining, and evolving with grace. This approach honors cycles instead of ladders, grace instead of grind. It mirrors the natural rhythm of expansion, allowing women to evolve without burnout. What began as intuition soon revealed itself as intelligence, a pattern waiting to be named.

The more I worked with women, the more I saw my own spiritual practice mirrored in their transformation. The same principles that grounded me through yoga philosophy, the Yamas and Niyamas, the Eight Limbs, and the discipline of self-study, began showing up in my coaching work. What I had practiced on the mat was preparing me to teach off it.

Every story in this book so far has been about moving *from chaos to clarity*. The archetypes helped name the chaos; the system gives it order. Understanding your archetype awakens self-awareness, but understanding the system awakens mastery. It's the difference between healing once and healing well.

This next phase of our journey shifts from healing to leadership, from knowing yourself to guiding others through your example. What healed you can heal many. Your transformation becomes timeless when it's supported by structure. That's what The Spiral Path represents: evolution made sustainable.

The framework that emerged from years of coaching, teaching, and spiritual study became something much more comprehensive. I began to see that women were breaking cycles, and they were building systems of sovereignty. **The Spiral**

Path captures that rhythm of transformation, blending ancient philosophy with modern strategy.

Each of the eight elements that follow mirrors the movement from inherited patterns to conscious creation. They guide you through the full arc of becoming: from awareness to embodiment, from discipline to devotion, from peace to power. Together, they form a map for sustained freedom. One that doesn't simply transform your life but also creates ripple effects across generations.

That repeating rhythm became what I now call **The Spiral Path**: the *method*, the *system*, the invisible architecture of lasting transformation. It is the internal engine that makes healing sustainable instead of temporary.

Over time, this method grew beyond theory. I refined it, layered it with yogic philosophy, integrated the Eight Limbs, and wove in the spiritual and emotional practices that shaped my life. The Spiral Path evolved into a complete and embodied journey, a full identity ascension framework. That evolution became my signature methodology: **The Luxe Identity Spiral™**.

The Spiral Path is the structure. The Luxe Identity Spiral™ is the experience. One is the method. The other is the lifestyle.

Together, they create a rhythmic, soulful system designed to help women evolve with ease, clarity, and sustained freedom.

LUXENARY BRIDGE: Your Next Evolution

Thriving Theresa is not the woman who *got lucky*. She is the woman who decided that the patterns would end with her. She is what happens when awareness becomes alignment, and alignment becomes embodiment. She doesn't simply know what she deserves. She lives like she deserves it. Every day. In every choice. In every boundary.

But her arrival is not the ending. It's the initiation.

In the next chapter, you'll step into the deeper structure that makes Thriving Theresa's confidence sustainable. You'll meet **Refined Integrity** (Yamas), the first of the eight elements that shape **The Spiral Path**. This is where transformation stops being accidental and becomes intentional. Predictable. Repeatable. Teach-able.

You're not purely creating a better life. You're creating a new lineage.

REFLECTION PROMPTS (Thriving Theresa)

Use these prompts to deepen your embodiment of Thriving Theresa:

1. What would your daily life look like if you fully trusted your own power?

2. Which habits, routines, or mindset patterns feel like the "next level" version of you?

3. How would Thriving Theresa respond to challenges — emotionally, spiritually, and practically?

4. What relationships shift when you step into confidence without shrinking?

5. What new patterns do you want to create for future generations?

6. How will you celebrate your growth journey without losing connection to your family or cultural roots?

7. What legacy feels aligned for the woman you are becoming?

8. Who will thank you — now or in the future — for choosing to break the cycle?

DAWNISM

"You become Thriving Theresa by agreement, not by accident."

AFFIRMATIONS

I honor the woman I am becoming. I trust myself to rise, receive, and expand. I create new patterns with clarity and confidence. I walk in freedom, for myself and for my lineage.

PART TWO

THE SPIRAL PATH

This is where the pattern breaks.

"*Your truth needs practice, not permission.*"

DAWNISM

Dawn M. Rivers

Chapter 6
YOU'VE BEEN LYING TO YOURSELF AND CALLING IT KINDNESS

When Someone Else's Dream Is Not Yours

My stepfather always believed in me, even when I didn't see my own potential.

He never went to college, and I'm not sure he graduated from high school. He migrated north to Cleveland from Arkansas. He played baseball for a short time in the Negro Leagues, and when he married my mom, he became the official 'note writer' whenever I needed a letter sent to my teachers. He had the best penmanship.

He read everything and taught himself basic computer programming. We had personal computers before they became household items. For my entire life, he was the editor, then vice president, of the *Call & Post* newspaper, one of the oldest Black newspapers in America. He created sales ads, specialized columns, and characters who played and predicted "the numbers."

When I wanted to create my own newspaper as an elementary-aged child, he encouraged me and even printed it out at the *Call & Post* for me. He let me use the Betacam recorder when I made my own evening news program.

So when I was working on my master's degree, he wanted me to earn my PhD. I promised him that I would.

It took me four years to earn my library and information science degree by the age of twenty-eight, and another four years of graduate-level coursework to become a licensed school librarian. By this time, I had been going to school nonstop since I was five years old, attending three undergraduate colleges and my second master's program. I had two children, was married, and I was tired.

My stepfather was diagnosed with prostate cancer after already surviving a triple bypass, but the cancer had metastasized. He fought hard but eventually gave up the fight. I didn't want to let him down, even in death, but I couldn't do it. Earning my PhD was never my dream. It was his.

Eventually, I forgave myself and left it all behind. I chose honesty over obligation. I honor him now through my writing, storytelling, and work ethic. He worked for the *Call & Post* until his last breath in the hospital. He loved what he did, and he was known all over the city because of it.

Letting go of that promise was one of my first big lessons in refined integrity: telling the truth about what was mine to carry and what wasn't.

I saw the same pattern later in other areas of my life.

I once told my son I was quitting as the middle school cheerleading coach. He said, "Good, because all you did was complain." My mouth dropped open. And he was right. I had said yes out of obligation, not alignment.

That's the cost of inherited people-pleasing patterns: you look like you're doing the "right" thing on the outside, but inside, you're out of integrity with yourself.

THE INHERITED BLUEPRINT: The "Keep the Peace" Programming

For many of us, boundary work doesn't begin with self-help books or therapy sessions; it begins with unspoken family expectations.

In my home, boundaries weren't discussed directly. They were modeled through sacrifice, silence, and subtle compliance. My mother learned to "keep the peace" from her mother, and her mother before that. It wasn't malicious; it was survival.

In generations past, Black women were often taught that strength meant endurance; that being agreeable kept families intact; that the measure of a good woman was how much she could carry without complaint.

But when peacekeeping becomes a reflex, truth is often the casualty. We learn to smile when we want to cry; say yes when our soul is screaming no; equate love with self-erasure. Those patterns run deep. They get coded into our nervous systems and passed down as "normal."

I watched the women in my family and my friends' families work tirelessly, rarely resting, often neglecting their own needs to meet everyone else's. Their worth was tied to their ability to serve. If they spoke up, they risked being labeled difficult or ungrateful. And so, like many daughters, I learned to perform: pleasing, perfecting, and overproducing my way through life.

That performance followed me into adulthood, shaping every career decision, relationship, and leadership role I stepped into.

What I didn't understand at first was that people-pleasing is a quiet form of dishonesty. It's a distortion of truth masked as kindness. When we say yes out of guilt, fear, or obligation, we betray our own integrity, and the cycle continues.

Awakening isn't loud. It's the moment you stop abandoning yourself.

Breaking that cycle means confronting the fear that honesty will cost us connection. It means unlearning cultural scripts that confuse compliance with compassion. And for women especially, it means reclaiming the right to exist in full truth without apology.

When I started honoring my limits instead of pushing past them, I began to see boundary work not as rebellion but as reverence—for my peace, my lineage, and my purpose.

True integrity doesn't demand perfection; it asks for alignment. Every time we choose alignment over approval, we rewrite the story our ancestors couldn't tell.

The Yamas Taught Me What Integrity Really Costs

Now that you see the patterns, let's talk about the FIRST pattern every cycle-breaker must face: boundaries.

The first step toward refined integrity is realizing that honesty isn't only about words; it's about energetic alignment.

In yoga philosophy, the Yamas are considered the ethical foundations of a conscious life. The two most relevant to boundary work are:

- *Satya* – truthfulness

- *Ahimsa* – non-harm

At first glance, these seem simple: tell the truth, and don't cause harm. But when we begin to live them in practice, we realize they can sometimes seem to conflict.

For instance, what happens when your truth might hurt someone you love? Or when silence feels like self-betrayal? This is the *paradox* that so many of us face.

In my own life, I've learned that the balance lies not in choosing one over the other, but in allowing both to *coexist*. Truth delivered with love heals. Honesty grounded in compassion liberates.

Integrity is about doing what's "right," and it's about staying aligned with your highest self. Every choice we make either strengthens or weakens that alignment. The moment we ignore our inner voice to maintain appearances or avoid conflict, we step out of integrity. Over time, that disconnection becomes emotional exhaustion, resentment, and self-doubt.

Generationally, many of us were taught to prioritize harmony over honesty. Our parents and grandparents often had to choose safety over self-expression, especially in environments where their voices were not welcomed. So they swallowed their truth to survive. That conditioning is powerful.

But survival-based patterns are not meant to lead a thriving life.

Thriving requires courage:

- the courage to speak truth even when your voice trembles

- the courage to rest when the world expects production

- the courage to honor your boundaries even when others misunderstand

In yoga, *Satya* and *Ahimsa* work together to create wholeness. Truth without compassion becomes cruelty; compassion without truth becomes enabling.

The art of living with integrity is learning how to honor both.

When we are honest with ourselves, we stop pretending that people-pleasing is kindness. When we practice non-harm, we stop weaponizing our truth as a form of control or superiority.

Living in refined integrity means your internal world and external actions are in harmony. You no longer apologize for your truth; you embody it. You no longer fear disappointing others; you focus on not disappointing your soul. And when that happens, an incredible freedom unfolds.

Generational healing begins here: when one person in a lineage decides to live in truth, the entire system begins to shift. Your children, your friends, even your colleagues, learn that honesty and love can coexist. Boundaries become an act of peace, not punishment. Saying no becomes sacred. Saying yes becomes powerful.

When I started to teach this principle to my clients, I saw the transformation immediately. Once they understood that setting a boundary was not rejection but refinement, their energy shifted. Their relationships either evolved or dissolved, but either way, peace followed.

Integrity creates a frequency of safety. People feel it when they are around you because you no longer operate from hidden motives or guilt. You say what you mean and mean what you say, and that vibration invites respect.

That is how truth becomes a healing force.

Refined integrity isn't about perfection; it's about alignment with divine truth. When we stop lying to ourselves to make others comfortable, we finally start living.

HOW EACH ARCHETYPE EXPERIENCES THIS

Stagnant Stella

For Stella, boundaries feel like confrontation. She was raised to keep the peace, to smooth things over, and to avoid "making a scene." She often says yes because she's afraid of what will happen if she says no. Her decisions come from a place of guilt, fear, or duty rather than truth.

She feels exhausted but believes that exhaustion is proof of love.

When she finally reaches her limit, it comes out in passive-aggressive comments or quiet resentment. Deep down, Stella doesn't trust that she can be loved and still have limits. She believes her value lies in her usefulness. Every time she overextends, she loses a little more of herself.

In her relationships, she tends to attract people who take more than they give, not because she's weak, but because she's unpracticed in receiving. *Stella's lesson in refined integrity is to recognize that peacekeeping without honesty is self-abandonment.* Her healing begins when she starts telling the truth: first to herself, then to others.

Searching Serena

Serena has started doing the work. She's reading the books, listening to the podcasts, and even journaling about boundaries. She's aware that people-pleasing doesn't serve her anymore, yet she still struggles to embody new patterns.

Her yes and no often fluctuate depending on her mood, confidence level, or fear of missing out. One week she's firm; the next, she's compromising again. She overcommits out of habit, then withdraws when burnout sets in.

Serena often confuses flexibility with a lack of structure. She tells herself she's being "easygoing," but she's really avoiding the discomfort that comes with enforcing her boundaries. She wants to be seen as kind, supportive, and helpful (qualities she truly possesses), but she's learning that kindness without self-respect isn't love.

For Serena, integrity work means creating internal consistency. When her word becomes her bond, not out of obligation but out of authenticity, her energy stabilizes. Her relationships shift from obligation to mutual respect.

Her mantra becomes: **"I can love you and still say no."**

Thriving Theresa

Theresa embodies refined integrity with grace. She's learned that honesty and kindness are not opposites; they are partners. Her boundaries are clear, loving, and firm. She no longer explains or defends her decisions because she trusts herself.

When she says yes, it's wholehearted. When she says no, it's final but gentle. She honors her commitments without sacrificing her peace.

Theresa's family and friends may not always understand her choices, especially if they're still caught in older patterns of self-sacrifice, but her consistency eventually teaches them something new. They start to see that boundaries create deeper trust, not distance.

In her business and personal life, Theresa leads with transparency. She practices what she preaches. Integrity has become her brand.

Theresa's presence naturally inspires others to elevate their own. *She shows that freedom doesn't come from pleasing everyone; it comes from living in truth.* Her version of luxury isn't material; it's emotional clarity. She sleeps well at night because her yes means yes, her no means no, and her heart stays open either way.

LUXE LIFESTYLE RITUAL: The Generational Boundary Audit

Boundaries are not barriers; they are bridges to freedom.

When you decide to live with refined integrity, your first task is to look at where your boundaries came from. The Generational Boundary Audit is a sacred reflection practice designed to help you see your inherited limits and create new standards that honor your truth.

Step 1: Map the Family Patterns

Take a blank sheet of paper or open your journal. Write the names of the women in your lineage: your mother, grandmother, great-grandmother, aunties, and even spiritual mothers. For each one, ask:

- How did she express her needs?

- How did she handle conflict?

- What did she sacrifice in the name of love or loyalty?

You may notice that boundary issues were not only personal but cultural. Many women were never given permission to say no. They were expected to carry everyone's burdens and smile through it. As you write, honor their strength without inheriting their silence.

Step 2: Identify the People-Pleasing Programs

Now, turn inward. Notice where those patterns still live in you.

- Do you overextend yourself to be liked?

- Do you soften your truth to avoid rejection?

- Do you take responsibility for everyone's comfort but your own?

Write down three areas of your life where this shows up: work, relationships, family, or even social media. Awareness is your liberation.

Step 3: Create New Boundary Standards

Ask yourself: What does integrity look like for me now?

Create a new code of conduct that aligns with your current values. It may include statements like:

- "I will no longer say yes when I mean no."

- "I will give from overflow, not depletion."

- "I will rest before I break."

Let these become your internal commandments.

Step 4: Practice Saying No with Love

The most luxurious boundary is a peaceful no.

Practice it in real life. Start small: decline an invitation that doesn't align, pause before committing, or take time to respond instead of reacting. When you say no with love, you are saying yes to peace.

This ritual isn't soley about behavior; it's about energetic reprogramming. As you honor your truth, your body begins to trust you again. You stop betraying yourself for acceptance and start radiating a calm, confident energy that says, *"I know who I am, and I choose peace."*

PATTERN RECOGNITION BOX

As I deepened my own boundary work, I started to notice how everything was connected. Every financial decision, every relationship dynamic, every energy leak traced back to integrity.

- When I overcommitted, money felt tight.

- When I said yes out of guilt, my body felt heavy.

- When I ignored my intuition, chaos followed.

Integrity is the root frequency of alignment. Without it, we repeat the same cycles under new names: different job, same stress; new partner, same pattern.

Boundaries are the quiet protectors of evolution. They guard your peace while your new identity takes form.

The moment you realize that boundary work isn't simply emotional but generational, everything changes. You begin to see how unspoken family rules shaped your nervous system and how your yes or no carries ancestral weight.

And then something miraculous happens. You stop seeing boundaries as selfish and start seeing them as sacred. Each one becomes a declaration of wholeness; a promise to the generations before you and the ones yet to come that the cycle of silence ends here.

Refined integrity isn't about control; it's about congruence. Once you live in alignment, you'll feel peace in places where you once felt pressure.

Before a Searching Serena can step into her next identity, she has to face the first and most uncomfortable part of evolution: *truth.* Awareness shows you the pattern, but integrity breaks it. Celeste learned that clarity means nothing without boundaries, and emotional insight means little without honest self-leadership. Every Seeking Woman eventually arrives at the same question: *Now that I know better, how do I live better?*

And this is where the real cycle-breaking begins; not in dramatic moments, but in the quiet, courageous act of telling the truth. The next chapter begins with that truth: refined integrity.

LUXENARY BRIDGE: Your Next Evolution

Your transition into the next spiral point

Next, you'll step into **Luxury Rituals** (Niyama), where integrity becomes embodied in your daily life. You've learned to tell the truth about what is and isn't yours to carry. Now you'll learn to build the sacred structures that protect what you've reclaimed. This is the evolution where self-care stops being an afterthought and becomes the architecture of your new identity.

In the next chapter, you'll discover that the Niyamas, the personal observances of yoga philosophy, are not simply wellness practices. They are the daily declarations of a woman who has decided she is worth tending to.

REFLECTION PROMPTS (Refined Integrity)

Use these prompts to deepen your work with this chapter:
1. Where do you still tell half-truths to keep the peace?

2. What inherited expectations are you carrying that were never truly yours?

3. Where does your body tighten or collapse when you're out of integrity?

4. What conversation have you been avoiding because you fear disappointing someone?

5. What would a loving, grounded "no" look like this week?

6. Which relationships shift when you show up honestly instead of performing?

7. What boundary would protect your peace right now, even if it feels uncomfortable?

8. Who are you becoming when you choose alignment over approval?

DAWNISM

"Your truth needs practice, not permission."

AFFIRMATIONS

I honor my truth with love and steadiness. I release the pressure to perform who I am not. My boundaries are acts of self-respect, not self-defense. I walk in alignment with clarity, courage, and calm.

> # *Your rituals are reminders of who you're finally becoming.*

DAWNISM

Dawn M. Rivers

Chapter 7

YOUR MOTHER NEVER RESTED. THAT STOPS WITH YOU.

What you learned from watching her

Memories of my mom growing up were of a woman who barely smiled. She looked unhappy and dissatisfied. She never spoke of it but it was always there. She was a smoker like her mother and aunts before her. When she was worried, she smoked. When she was angry, she smoked. When she talked on the phone, she smoked. Then when I was in junior high school she gave up smoking. I was proud of her for making a bold and difficult choice to end a habit she had for decades. That was the first time I saw her take her health into her hands.

But she didn't stop there. She started taking aerobics at a women's health center near our house. My mom loved it. She went for a long time, but when they closed she didn't look for a new place to continue her fitness journey. It seemed like she lost something she loved.

Whatever my mom was looking for she never seemed to find it. She would shop with my great aunt and they would go to flea markets, antique stores, and estate sales. This went on for years until my great aunt slipped and was afraid of going out because she might fall. She did try shopping with friends but it wasn't as fun because they were in competition for antiques. Then when I came home with a baby from college, I became my mother's shopping buddy. This was her way of bonding with me.

However, my mom never went back to real self care. Before my stepfather got sick, vacationing was her obsession. The two of them went on a cruise with friends and eventually purchased two timeshares in Florida and would trade in one to vacation in different states. My family accompanied them and we loved it. We went to Florida for at least ten years straight. My stepfather and I loved Disney World and went as many times as we could before my mom urged that we explore other places.

When my stepfather got sick and could no longer travel the way we did, my mom became depressed again. And when he passed away, she lost her ability to walk. Seriously, she had to use a cane to get around the house. Her fear and anxiety caused her body to freeze up. She suffered from fibromyalgia. That led her to take steroids which led to other complications. Her health suffered for a few years.

I had divorced my husband, sent my son off to college, celebrated my daughter's graduation with honors, and was putting my life back together. I was practicing yoga almost daily, created Daybreak Yoga LLC, and made my first ever vision board. Things were coming together for me, and fast. I was traveling solo, enjoying events around the city, and taking risks.

That next year, my mom decided to go to Cancun for the month of February after she saw me checking things off my list. She wanted to try this. She had finally gotten back to herself and I was extremely elated for her. This was a big step and I wanted to support her when she asked me if I could come down for a few days while she was there. I was able to get additional days off from work surrounding an extended weekend at school. (Again, things were working out for me and fast!) We had a great time together. Of course she wanted to shop, but I convinced her to go to a museum and to see the pyramids. When I had to leave, she was sad but she stayed for the rest of the month.

She used her timeshare to plan this trip as well as trips to celebrate my children graduating from college. My mom even began planning for us to return to Florida. This was difficult for her because it was strongly tied to memories of my stepfather. The thrill of seeing more of the world was swelling up within her. She took trips with friends to Myrtle Beach, Hawaii, the Poconos, and other places.

But then she had a stroke that affected her eyesight and she gave up completely. After being released from the hospital, she didn't want to go to a rehabilitation facility or the sight center to learn how to manage her diminished vision. When she complained of back pain, she quit going to physical therapy because it was hard. When she didn't like the aides who helped, she fired them. Her words continued to be, "I just want to die."

When my grandmother broke her hip, her heart was only functioning at twenty-five percent, and within days of her being hospitalized, she died. We never talked about it so I don't really know more than that. This seems to be a common occurrence in Black households. We don't share the family stories and struggles, so our children and grandchildren never really know their history.

I was determined to be healthy and take better care of myself. It started when I began to eliminate meat from my diet. Someone from my yoga class gave me a book that I can't find anywhere, called something like "From Health to Super Health." It talked about how much energy the body uses to digest meat. It takes hours and uses up the energy that could go to the brain and other organs. I decided then to start eating differently. I was ridiculed by my husband and was misunderstood by many others, but I felt amazing. I continued to make changes and prioritize my self care: I took long baths, drank gallons of water every month, and laughed more. My body started to feel better. No more migraines, back pain, and excess mucus. It was remarkable.

As I got older, I didn't practice power yoga anymore but started to embrace slow flow practices and Yin Yoga. I began to listen to my body more and prioritize rest. I was tired. I remember taking naps on the storytime carpet in the school library during my lunch break. That's when I started to incorporate digital detoxes: no tv, no computers, no cellphone, no radio, no electronics at all. I even walked to work.

I saw what was happening to the women around me and consciously decided to take care of me. This went well for me for years until I became my mother's caregiver and suffered from vertigo and low blood pressure. I lost myself in trying to convince my mother she needed to take care of herself. Slowly but surely I was losing myself in stress and depression again.

Because of the grief of closing my yoga studio, I stopped practicing yoga. I sat for hours on end "hustling" in my coaching business. The entrepreneurs I followed endorsed this mentality and I felt like if I wasn't working hard, then I was failing. I was slipping away and had forgotten who I was and what I had done. So I went back to yoga, meditation and breathing exercises. I went back to taking long baths and using essential oils. I went back to taking naps, digital detoxes, and walking more. Self-care isn't self-indulgent. It's self-preservation. To me, self care is an aspect of the divine feminine.

THE INHERITED BLUEPRINT: The Lineage of Self-Neglect and Overwork

In many families, especially among Black women, self-care has long been treated as a luxury rather than a right. We watched our mothers and grandmothers push through pain, hide their exhaustion, and sacrifice their joy for survival. They had to be both provider and protector. They cloaked themselves in masculinity. Rest was often seen as laziness, pleasure as indulgence, and asking for help as weakness. What began as resilience became routine. What started as strength turned into self-neglect.

My mother was like so many women of her generation battling with depression. She did her best to raise my brother and me alone until she married my stepfather. She earned her bachelor degree in business, worked for the city government, and put us in activities. She didn't know how to manage her unhappiness or deal with my stepfather's drunken rages. She worked hard, kept the house running, and rarely paused to nurture herself. When she did find something that brought her joy, like aerobics or travel, life circumstances or guilt eventually pulled her away from it. Somewhere along the way, she forgot what it felt like to simply *feel good*.

These patterns don't disappear with time; they shape us. As daughters, we internalize what we witness. We learn to equate productivity with worth, exhaustion with success, and martyrdom with meaning. Even when we rebel outwardly, the body remembers those old lessons. We may call it ambition, dedication, or drive, but underneath it often lies inherited anxiety: the fear that stillness will make us irrelevant or unloved.

Breaking that cycle requires courage. It means refusing to carry what isn't ours. It means honoring the body as sacred, not as a machine. It means redefining what luxury really is: not diamonds and designer bags, but discipline, devotion, and deep care.

There's a generational guilt that surfaces when we begin to care for ourselves differently. Part of us feels like we're betraying our lineage, like we've forgotten the women who couldn't rest because they were too busy surviving. But the truth is, self-care isn't betrayal; it's continuation. It's what they prayed for, even if they didn't have the language to say it.

When I take a nap, light a candle, or sit quietly with my tea, I'm not being selfish; I'm finishing a sentence they never got to complete. Every act of care is a small rebellion against a culture that glorifies hustle and struggle. And every time we choose peace over pressure, we rewrite what our daughters will one day call normal.

The Niyamas Taught Me That Rest Is Revolutionary

The heart of *Niyama* is personal observance: the daily disciplines that keep us anchored in alignment. If the **Yamas** teach us how to relate *ethically* to the world, the **Niyamas** teach us how to relate *lovingly* to ourselves. They are the foundations of self-respect, and when practiced consistently, they become the quiet rituals that transform ordinary days into sacred experiences.

In yoga philosophy, Niyamas include purity, contentment, discipline, self-study, and devotion to the Divine. Each one reminds us that **inner order creates outer harmony**. For many of us, especially women raised to give endlessly, these practices are radical acts of remembrance. They teach us that caring for the self is not vanity; it's vitality.

When I first started studying yoga, I saw self-care as something to check off a list. Drink water. Stretch. Meditate. But as I matured, I realized that rituals are not habits; they are conversations with the soul. True luxury is rhythmic, not rushed. It's devotion disguised as discipline.

The mistake many people make is thinking that transformation comes from grand gestures. In truth, the most powerful shifts happen through small, consistent actions. Lighting incense before prayer. Stretching before bed. Writing gratitude in the morning. These simple moments create energetic order. **They train the nervous system to associate stillness with safety and joy with worthiness.**

When we neglect these small practices, we unconsciously replay the patterns of our lineage: overworking, overgiving, and overlooking our needs. Generational self-neglect shows up as busyness, martyrdom, and burnout. It tells us we don't have time to care for ourselves, when in reality, we can't afford not to.

One of my favorite teachings from the Yoga Sutras says that self-discipline (**Tapas**) burns away impurities. Tapas isn't punishment or restriction; it's the inner fire that keeps you awake to your purpose. Every morning you rise with intention, you feed that fire. Every time you choose rest over rushing, you honor that fire. Every act of care becomes a declaration that you belong to yourself.

Luxury rituals aren't about extravagance; they're about consistency. They bring grace to structure. They remind us that we don't have to hustle for worthiness. When practiced over time, these rituals shift your frequency. You begin to feel more grounded, centered, and clear. Life starts to respond differently because you're living differently.

Your rituals are the rhythm your children will remember. They'll see what peace looks like. They'll watch how you move through stress with presence instead of panic. They'll learn that self-care is not indulgence but inheritance.

Every bath, every journal entry, every mindful breath is a love letter to the generations before you who never got the chance. Ritual is remembrance. Routine becomes reverence. And in that sacred repetition, new lineage begins.

HOW EACH ARCHETYPE EXPERIENCES THIS

Stagnant Stella

Stella rarely puts herself first. She's been taught that her worth is measured by how much she does for others, not how well she cares for herself. When she does take a moment to rest, guilt quickly follows. Her to-do list never ends, and she wears exhaustion like a badge of honor. Self-care feels optional, even selfish. Deep down, she longs to slow down but doesn't trust that life will keep moving if she does.

Her mornings often start in chaos: checking her phone, answering messages, and running on caffeine and adrenaline. She collapses into bed at night wondering why she feels unfulfilled even when she's accomplished so much. Stella's body keeps score: fatigue, migraines, inflammation, anxiety. Her healing begins when she understands that rest is not weakness but wisdom. For her, *creating a morning ritual might start with something as simple as silence before sunrise or gratitude before scrolling.* The more she practices stillness, the safer it feels.

Searching Serena

Serena knows the value of self-care. She's tried every morning routine trending online: lemon water, journaling, dry brushing, ten-step skincare. Her Pinterest boards are full of rituals that look beautiful but feel hard to maintain. She starts strong and fades fast because her motivation is rooted in performance, not peace.

Serena still carries the generational guilt of wanting more ease than her mother ever allowed herself. She feels torn between honoring her ambition and slowing down enough to enjoy it. Her pattern is inconsistency. Some days she's all in; others, she abandons her rituals completely when life gets busy. The deeper work for Serena is not about adding more. It's about simplifying. *When she finds the practices that truly nourish her, she realizes consistency doesn't require perfection.* It requires presence. Self-care becomes sustainable when it aligns with her real life, not her ideal one.

Thriving Theresa

Theresa's life flows in rhythm with her rituals. Her mornings are intentional, not hurried. She begins each day with gratitude, hydration, stillness, and movement. These aren't chores; they're her compass. She's learned that her energy is her most valuable currency, and her rituals protect it.

Theresa embodies the truth that discipline is devotion. She's not rigid, but she's rooted. When she travels or her schedule shifts, she adapts rather than abandons her structure. Her rituals are flexible frameworks, not cages. Her home, workspace, and body reflect her values of balance, beauty, and peace. The people around her feel her calm confidence; her presence gives permission for others to rest.

Theresa's version of luxury isn't about expensive products but the energy of ease she brings to everything she touches. *Her rituals are her revolution*; they represent generations of women who couldn't rest, but now she does. Through her example, luxury becomes legacy.

LUXE LIFESTYLE RITUAL: Design Your Legacy Morning

Every morning is an invitation to rewrite your lineage. The way you rise sets the rhythm for your day, but more importantly, it redefines what "normal" feels like in your body. Designing a **Legacy Morning** isn't about perfection or productivity; it's about presence, appreciation, and intention.

Step 1: Break the Pattern

Look at how mornings have traditionally felt in your family. Were they rushed, loud, stressful, or disconnected? Maybe everyone scrambled to get out the door, or maybe mornings were filled with silence that felt heavy. Your first act of healing is to choose differently. Before you reach for your phone or start checking boxes, pause. Place your hand on your heart and whisper, "I get to begin again."

Step 2: Include What Your Ancestors Couldn't Access

Think about what your mother or grandmother didn't have time or space to do. Maybe she wanted to stretch, sip coffee slowly, or journal by the window. Add one of those rituals to your morning. It doesn't have to take long. Two minutes of mindful breathing or writing a single page of reflection can honor generations who didn't have that privilege.

Step 3: Build Your Morning Around Appreciation

Before doing anything external, practice gratitude. List three things that feel good in your life right now. Gratitude anchors you in abundance. Follow it with one action that nourishes your body: hydrating, stretching, or walking outside. Let the body feel your thankfulness.

Step 4: Make It Sustainable

A Legacy Morning isn't built on pressure; it's built on rhythm. Create something you can maintain, not something you'll abandon after a week. If you have ten minutes, that's enough. The key is consistency over intensity. Let your routine evolve with you.

Step 5: Add Beauty and Intention

Light a candle. Play soft music. Use your favorite cup. These small touches shift your nervous system and signal to your subconscious that your life is sacred.

When you start your mornings this way, you send a new message to your lineage: rest is safe, pleasure is sacred, and structure can be soft. This ritual becomes your daily declaration that you are no longer surviving; you are choosing to live luxuriously, one morning at a time.

PATTERN RECOGNITION BOX

As I deepened my self-care rituals, I started to see how my relationship with structure revealed my deeper patterns. The way I treated my mornings mirrored how I treated my life. If I rushed through the first hour of the day, I rushed through the rest. If I started with gratitude, the whole day flowed in ease.

The truth is, our daily rituals expose our generational scripts. If your mother or grandmother moved through life in constant motion, chances are you inherited her pace. You may feel guilty resting because she never could. You may feel anxious slowing down because chaos feels familiar. These are not personal flaws; they're inherited patterns.

When we pause to create rituals of care, we interrupt those old rhythms. *We remind the body that stillness is not danger; it's safety.* That joy is not frivolous; it's fuel. That consistency is not control; it's devotion.

Rituals reveal where we've been repeating and where we're ready to rewrite.

They show us that the luxury we seek isn't outside of us; it's in the way we tend to what's already here. Once you see this pattern clearly, every choice becomes sacred.

LUXENARY BRIDGE: Your Next Evolution

Your transition into the next spiral point

Luxury Rituals (Niyama) is where self-care becomes self-respect. It's where you stop performing strength and start practicing softness, where you stop carrying the weight of your lineage and begin tending to yourself the way they never could. This chapter marks the moment you realize: tending to your body, your energy, and your rhythm is not indulgence. It's inheritance.

But this is only the beginning.

When you consistently pour into yourself, something powerful awakens. Your posture shifts. Your presence grounds. Your confidence becomes embodied rather than imagined. This is the next evolution: **the woman whose body tells the truth of her healing.**

In the next chapter, you'll step into **Embodied Confidence (Asana)**. The place where self-care becomes sovereignty, where your physical presence mirrors your inner alignment, and where you begin to live your truth through the body, breath, and nervous system.

REFLECTION PROMPTS (Luxury Rituals)

Use these prompts to deepen your awakening into personal observance:

1. When you reflect on the women in your family, how did they relate to rest, pleasure, or slowing down?

2. Where does your body show signs of inherited self-neglect (fatigue, tension, guilt when resting)?

3. What old beliefs about rest or self-care still live inside you, and whose voice do they sound like?

4. Which rituals already nourish you, even if you practice them inconsistently?

5. What would a simplified, sustainable ritual look like if it were built around your *real* life (not your idealized one)?

6. Where do you confuse hustling with worthiness or chaos with productivity?

7. What ritual could you commit to for the next seven days that feels gentle, grounding, and doable?

8. What new definition of "luxury" feels true for the woman you're becoming?

DAWNISM

"Your rituals are reminders of who you're finally becoming."

AFFIRMATIONS

I honor my body with rhythm, not pressure. I choose consistency over perfection, presence over performance. My self-care is a sacred inheritance and a living legacy. I am worthy of rest, replenishment, and radical devotion.

> # *Your body tells the truth long before your words do.*

DAWNISM

Dawn M. Rivers

Chapter 8

STAND UP STRAIGHT. YOUR ANCESTORS ARE WATCHING.

Your Body Has Been Trying to Tell You Something

It was 1986, I was a junior in high school and had been studying Spanish for four years starting in eighth grade. Now I had the opportunity to participate in an exchange program through my high school in Mexico. I was excited and couldn't wait to go. But my mom said no, I couldn't travel to Mexico. I was devastated, down, and disappointed.

I learned later that my mom was afraid for me to go to Mexico even though school exchange and study abroad programs had been around for decades. When I went to college I didn't think about doing a semester abroad in a Spanish speaking country. I didn't know that was a possibility for me. I was sheltered and ignorant. Plus I was unfocused and unmotivated. Really, I was totally unprepared for college all together.

Decades later when I was a high school librarian, the Asian studies program coordinator said he and his colleague had been watching me interact with the students, observing how I carried myself, and would love for me to take students to Japan. I was shocked and surprised but fearful. I asked if I could have a couple of days to talk to my family. My husband was on board but again my mother was fearful.

I would be gone for a month that summer and would have to coordinate my children's activities around their firefighter father's 24-hour work shifts. My good friend, Wendy, who is my children's godmother, stepped in to help. With my parents, in-laws and her, I figured out a solution for my children when their dad was working. I told the Asian Studies program coordinators I was in and was honored to be asked to go!

This trip changed my life. I loved Japan and my host family was generous and gracious. I was in awe of the ancient cities, culture, and customs. When we returned home, I was ready to incorporate what I learned into both my personal and professional lives. Japan helped me walk through the streets with my head up, shoulders back, all in high heels.

After this trip, the next year I was asked to take students to Mexico City for two weeks. Then I wrapped up my high school librarianship with a month in Germany on another student exchange. And when I was a middle school librarian, I was selected by the State Department to serve as an educational ambassador to Brazil for two and a half weeks.

I turned my mother's and my fears into fearlessness.

The trip to Brazil was a lesson on fierceness. The program assigned the applicants to a country they selected for them, but I decided I wanted to go to Brazil and not leave it up to chance. I "claimed" my spot in the program and decided that I would travel to Brazil. I spoke about it to the coordinators and teachers when they came to my school. I wrote what I would do in Brazil when I went. I even said why it would benefit my current school community and students for me to go to Brazil. So when they announced the teachers who were accepted and which countries they would be sent to, they chose Brazil for me. The director said I had made a compelling case for myself so of course they were sending me to Brazil!

My mom's world viewpoint was influenced by the violent acts of racism against students who dared to speak up or step outside of the societal norms created by systematic oppression. During her high school and college years, students were arrested, harassed, and even lynched. Therefore her fears were founded. And because of her generation's sacrifices, our school systems have made positive strides toward equality and equanimity. I think, my mom was strategic and specific about where my brother and I attended school.

As my friend and yoga colleague, Koya Webb, says, "Let your fears make you fierce." Every school exchange I took with students or solo trips I ventured on, my body stood taller with my shoulders back and heart open ready to receive what the experience had to offer me.

THE INHERITED BLUEPRINT: The Body That Learned to Hold Trauma for Generations

For generations, women, especially Black women, have been told to shrink. To be polite, modest, and invisible enough to stay safe. We were taught to blend in, not stand out; to serve, not shine. That conditioning seeps into the body before we even realize it. The shoulders curl inward, the breath gets shallow, and the posture of protection becomes the posture of identity.

My mother carried herself with quiet dignity, but also with an invisible weight. I watched her body speak even when her mouth didn't. Her steps were careful, her tone measured, her presence small. She didn't walk into a room; she slipped into it. Her fear was inherited, too, passed down through stories of survival, scarcity, and social expectation. And like so many daughters, I absorbed that message without words: *It's safer to stay small.*

Shrinking isn't always physical; sometimes it's emotional or energetic. It shows up when we silence ourselves in meetings, minimize our achievements, or apologize for existing too boldly. Our lineage teaches us to equate safety with invisibility, but what if that lesson has expired?

The truth is, the body keeps score of what the mind suppresses. *Generational pain lives in memory and it lives in muscle.* It's the tight jaw, the tense shoulders, the clenching of the gut every time you're asked to be "less." These inherited patterns of contraction are not who we are; they're the echoes of who our mothers had to be.

Breaking that cycle means reclaiming the body as sacred ground. It's learning to take up space not in arrogance, but in authenticity. To stand tall, breathe fully, and move with presence. The act of expansion, lifting your chest, grounding your feet, opening your heart, becomes a declaration of healing.

Our ancestors endured what they had to endure so we could evolve. We honor them not by shrinking, but by standing. Every time we walk into a room without apology, we rewrite their story. Every time we breathe deeply and speak truth without trembling, we signal to our nervous system: *it's safe to be seen.*

What Asana Actually Means Off the Mat

The physical practice of yoga, *Asana,* is often misunderstood as stretching or exercise. But in truth, Asana is about posture in the fullest sense: the way you hold yourself in the world. It is about how the inner and outer body communicate alignment. The Yoga Sutras describe Asana as a state that is *"steady and comfortable,"* a harmony between strength and surrender.

When we practice being steady and comfortable in our physical body, we are teaching our nervous system that safety and strength can coexist. For women who grew up internalizing messages of shrinking, this is revolutionary. We are retraining the body to believe it can handle visibility, voice, and presence without danger.

Posture affects psychology. The way we sit, stand, and move sends signals to the brain about who we are. Shoulders back and heart open tell your subconscious, *I am safe. I belong here.* Shoulders slumped and gaze down tell it, *I need to hide.* For generations, our mothers and grandmothers learned to tuck their light behind closed doors to avoid being misunderstood, punished, or dismissed. That posture of survival became encoded as "normal."

When I began to study yoga deeply, I noticed that my body had its own history of contraction. My jaw tightened during conflict. My shoulders folded when I felt misunderstood. My hips stored years of unspoken grief. It was humbling to realize how much of my family's pain lived in my posture. I had been trying to think my way into confidence when what I really needed was to *feel* my way there.

Embodiment is where confidence becomes real. You can repeat affirmations all day, but until your body believes them, they don't land. Standing tall, breathing deeply, and moving intentionally are more than gestures; they're gateways. Each movement communicates to the cells, "We are no longer surviving; we are thriving."

This is why embodiment work is essential to generational healing. It interrupts the inherited patterns stored in the nervous system. It teaches the body that it can be seen without danger, hold boundaries without fear, and express joy without guilt.

When your physical body is aligned, your mental posture follows. You start walking differently, speaking differently, showing up differently. You stop apologizing for your presence and start celebrating it. You begin to realize that taking up space is not a threat; it's an offering.

Asana becomes an act of remembrance. You remember that your body is not a burden; it's your bridge to freedom. You remember that movement is medicine, and posture is prayer. You remember that confidence is not about control but about connection.

This is the invitation of **Embodied Confidence**: to inhabit your life fully, to let your body lead your healing, and to reclaim the physical presence your lineage lost. Each time you stand tall, you lift the generations that came before you. Each time you move with intention, you model freedom for the ones who will follow.

Your body is your testimony. Let it speak truth.

HOW EACH ARCHETYPE EXPERIENCES THIS

Stagnant Stella

Stella has spent years carrying the weight of other people's expectations. Her body tells her story before she speaks. Her shoulders slump from years of emotional labor, her back aches from unexpressed burdens, and her breath sits shallow in her chest. She rarely moves her body with joy. Exercise feels like punishment, not pleasure.

When Stella looks in the mirror, she often sees fatigue more than potential. She hides behind loose clothing, crossed arms, and polite smiles. Her energy says, "I'm fine," but her body whispers, "I'm tired." She's learned to make herself smaller to make others comfortable, to take up as little space as possible so she won't be seen as "too much."

Stella's breakthrough begins when she remembers that movement is a language, not a chore. A morning stretch, a walk in the sun, or even a deep breath at her desk becomes an act of rebellion. As she starts to feel safer in her body, she begins to stand taller. Her confidence doesn't arrive as loud declarations; it comes as quiet alignment.

Searching Serena

Serena knows that her body holds wisdom, but she still struggles to trust it. She's tried yoga, Pilates, gym memberships, and mirror affirmations, searching for something that sticks. She often moves from motivation to guilt, measuring her worth by the number on the scale or the number of workouts she completes.

Serena's relationship with embodiment is inconsistent. Some days she feels radiant and grounded; other days she avoids her reflection altogether. She still hears the voice of comparison: the one that tells her she should look or move differently. Deep down, she craves freedom in her body, but she hasn't learned how to anchor it yet.

Her evolution begins when she realizes that confidence isn't about control; it's about connection. When she practices movement that feels intuitive instead of performative, her self-criticism softens. She begins to move because it feels good, not because she's trying to prove something. The more she breathes into her body, the more her mind begins to trust it.

Thriving Theresa

Theresa moves through the world like her body is her altar. She walks with grounded grace, speaks with embodied ease, and treats her body like a sacred home. Years of intentional practice have taught her that posture is prayer and movement is gratitude. Her daily rituals— stretching, dancing, walking, resting—are acts of devotion.

Theresa doesn't chase confidence; she *is* confidence. She listens to her body's cues and responds with compassion. She's let go of the need for external validation because she's learned to source her power from within. Her energy commands attention without demanding it. When she enters a room, people feel her presence before she says a word.

For Theresa, *embodiment is leadership.* Her physical presence teaches others what freedom looks like. She models what happens when a woman stops apologizing for her existence and starts living in her full expression. Every movement, every breath, every step becomes a declaration: *I belong here. I am enough. I am free.*

LUXE LIFESTYLE RITUAL: The Ancestral Power Sequence

Your body remembers what your mind forgets. Every gesture, every breath, every flinch holds ancestral information. The **Ancestral Power Sequence** is a morning embodiment practice designed to release inherited tension, reawaken confidence, and remind your body that it is safe to take up space.

Step 1: Ground Through the Feet

Stand tall with your feet hip-width apart. Feel the earth beneath you. Spread your toes, root through your heels, and take a deep breath into your belly. Whisper to yourself, "I am grounded in my power."

This simple connection restores stability. Your ancestors may have had to stay ready to run: physically, emotionally, or spiritually. You get to stay *rooted*.

Step 2: Open the Heart Space

Place your hands over your chest and lift through your sternum as you breathe deeply. Roll your shoulders back slowly. Imagine every inhale expanding your courage and every exhale releasing inherited fear. Let the body soften without collapsing.

This movement opens the energetic space where confidence lives. The chest is where pride, worthiness, and voice intersect.

Step 3: Lift the Crown

Lengthen your spine and imagine a golden thread pulling from the crown of your head toward the sky. Let your chin level with the horizon. This is how you signal to the world, and your nervous system, that you're ready to be seen.

Step 4: Power Poses and Affirmations

Move through these three postures slowly, breathing deeply with each:
- **Warrior II:** "I stand firmly in who I am."

- **Mountain Pose:** "I am steady, strong, and supported."

- **Goddess Pose:** "I take up sacred space."
  Hold each for three to five breaths, feeling your strength rise with every inhale.

Step 5: Integration Practice

Close with a seated moment of stillness. Place your hands on your knees and feel the pulse of life within you. Say quietly, "This body carries generations of strength, and today, I honor it."

You don't need a mat or a full hour, five minutes of conscious embodiment shifts everything. When you move intentionally, you communicate to your lineage that survival is no longer the goal. Thriving is.

PATTERN RECOGNITION BOX

As I became more aware of my body, I started noticing patterns that weren't purely mine. The way I tensed my shoulders in conflict, clenched my teeth when anxious, or balling my fist in discomfort, these were inherited postures. They were learned behaviors disguised as body language.

Our families teach us how to inhabit space. Some teach expansion and ease, others teach containment and control. I realized that my own shrinking wasn't only emotional; it was physical. I had been carrying generations of women who were told to stay quiet, stay small, stay safe.

The body holds history, but it also holds the power to rewrite it. Every stretch, every full breath, every lifted chin is a declaration that the story ends differently here.

Embodied confidence is not vanity; it's truth expressed through motion. It's how the soul says, *I'm home now.* When I stand tall, I honor the women who couldn't. When I move freely, I remind my body that it belongs to joy, not fear.

That's when I understood: *embodiment isn't about mastering a pose; it's about mastering presence.* Once you reconnect with your body's wisdom, you'll never need permission to take up space again.

LUXENARY BRIDGE: Your Next Evolution

Your transition into the next spiral point

Embodied Confidence awakens a truth that goes far beyond the mat: once your body remembers its power, your life begins to mirror that posture. Standing tall becomes a habit. Speaking up becomes natural. Taking up space becomes sacred.

But embodiment is only one layer of liberation.

The next evolution asks a deeper question: **What happens when your *energy* becomes as aligned as your body?**

In the next chapter, you'll step into **Energetic Mastery**. The place where your breath, nervous system, and inner frequency create the foundation for clarity, peace, and presence. If Chapter 8 is about reclaiming your physical power, Chapter 9 is about learning to regulate the internal landscape that determines how you move through the world.

You've learned to stand tall. Now you'll learn to stay centered.

REFLECTION PROMPTS (Embodied Confidence)

Use these prompts to deepen your embodiment journey:

1. How did the women in your family carry themselves and what did their posture teach you about safety or visibility?

2. Where in your life do you still shrink to keep the peace or avoid attention?

3. When you speak your truth, what sensations arise in your body: tightness, release, warmth, trembling?

4. Which part of your body feels like it holds the most generational tension?

5. What would "taking up space" look like emotionally, spiritually, or socially not only physically?

6. When was the last time you felt powerful in your body? What triggered it, and how can you recreate it?

7. How does your breath change when you feel confident versus when you feel afraid?

8. Complete this sentence: **"In this body, I choose to..."**

DAWNISM

"Your body tells the truth long before your words do."

AFFIRMATIONS

I stand tall in the fullness of who I am. My breath grounds me in strength and grace.

I release inherited fear and embody freedom.I am safe, seen, and sovereign in my body.

> # "Change your breath; change your frequency."

DAWNISM

Dawn M. Rivers

Chapter 9

SHE SMOKED TO COPE. YOU'RE GOING TO BREATHE INSTEAD.

What you choose now changes everything after you

I had a contradictory viewpoint of smoking. I thought my mom looked cool smoking her Virginia Slims but I didn't like the way it smelled. My brother and I implored her, our great aunts and maternal grandmother to quit. When she finally did, I had a sense of relief. The surgeon general had made scary warnings about death and cancer related to cigarette smoking. There were even terrifying television commercials about the effects smoking had on the body. As a child I was worried for her wellbeing and didn't know how to help her.

Cigarette smoking was her way of soothing herself. If she had an argument with my stepfather, she smoked. If she had a stressful day at work, she smoked. If my brother and I upset her, she smoked. She smoked when she talked on the phone which I felt was nonstop. If my parents had their "grownup" parties in the basement where they played cards, danced, and drank, my brother and I could see the plumes of smoke wafting up from downstairs.

I didn't think my mom had any other coping skills that helped her with anxiety or depression. It was the 1970s, in Midwest America, suburban Cleveland, Ohio. I never heard of anyone practicing yoga, doing breathing exercises, or meditating. Folks stamped out their difficult times with drugs and alcohol. They "partied" on the weekends and went back to work on Monday.

The first time I learned a breathing technique was in power hot yoga. *Ujjayi* pranayama breath was the foundation of the practice. It's also known as victorious breath or sometimes it's called ocean breath. One deeply inhales through their nostrils while constricting the back of their throat causing the sound over the vocal cords to vibrate. As one gets more comfortable with the practice, they constrict the back of their throats during both the inhale and the exhale. An easy way to practice is to start by fogging up a mirror. The actions are similar. This technique is great for bringing the nervous system into a calm state. The parasympathetic nervous system sends signals to the body to relax.

When I would catch myself tensing up, clinching my teeth or making fists with my hands, I knew I needed to stop and breathe. It became a healing balm to my soul. Breath work has helped me stop and pause before making a decision, responding to someone, or being reactive. By no means do I always turn to breathwork when I have to make a quick decision, but I almost always do a breathing exercise to regroup and regulate myself.

When my adult children face challenges, I remind them to breathe. Square breath is the easiest one to do. They thank me for the reminder. So I know this is helping to create a shift in the generational patterns by using breathing exercises and other coping mechanisms to mitigate stress, anxiety, and depression.

THE INHERITED BLUEPRINT: The Nervous System Trained for Vigilance

Our families teach us how to breathe long before we ever become conscious of it. We learn their pace, their pauses, their sighs, and their silence. Breath carries more than oxygen. It carries emotion, memory, and history. For many of us, especially women raised in households where stress was constant, our nervous systems were shaped by the rhythm of survival.

In my family, breath was often shallow and hurried. My mother's cigarette breaks were her only pauses, her exhale wrapped in smoke and worry. Her breath wasn't rest; it was release. She inhaled anxiety and exhaled exhaustion. That was the only model she had for self-regulation, and in many ways, it became the template for mine.

This is how nervous system patterns are passed down: quietly, invisibly, through the way our families manage emotion. We inherit not only their stories but their stress responses. *The body remembers what the mind normalizes.* Hypervigilance becomes a habit, tension becomes tradition, and we call it "just how we are."

Generational anxiety isn't limited to the mental; it's cellular. When our mothers and grandmothers didn't have access to calm, they taught us to live on alert. They smoked, drank, or numbed because stillness felt unsafe. Their bodies were constantly preparing for the next problem, even when none existed. Over time, that vigilance became the family default; a pattern of holding the breath instead of using it.

Breaking that cycle begins with awareness, but healing it requires breath. Conscious breathing is the bridge between inherited pain and intentional peace. It interrupts the body's autopilot. It's the moment where reaction becomes response, and history becomes healing.

Each slow, steady inhale is an act of rebellion against the chaos that came before. Each exhale releases generations of tension stored in the body. Through breath, we remind our lineage that safety is possible, calm is accessible, and peace can be practiced.

When we breathe with awareness, we teach our children that calm is not the absence of conflict; it's the presence of control. We stop passing down panic and start passing down peace. Breath becomes the new inheritance.

Pranayama Gave Me What My Mother Never Had

Breath is the bridge between the seen and unseen, the physical and the spiritual, the past and the present. In yoga philosophy, *Pranayama* means the expansion and regulation of life force energy. It teaches that your breath is more than an automatic process; it's a tool for mastery. When you control the breath, you influence the mind. When you influence the mind, you transform your energy.

Most of us grew up unaware of this power. We were taught to suppress emotions, to "keep it together," to calm down without being shown *how*. The nervous system of a woman who was never taught to breathe is one that survives, not one that thrives. This is why the cycles of anxiety and reactivity repeat generation after generation, because the body has never been shown another way to feel safe.

Breathwork changes that. Each inhale is a conscious invitation to be present; each exhale is a conscious act of release. When you begin to observe your breathing patterns, you're observing your energy patterns. Do you hold your breath when you're anxious? Do you exhale quickly when you're frustrated? Do you sigh deeply when you're overwhelmed? Your breath reveals your emotional landscape.

In yoga, the breath is considered the first form of alignment. You can't balance the body if the breath is chaotic. You can't still the mind if the breath is shallow. Breath anchors awareness, connecting you back to your inner rhythm instead of your inherited one.

The Yoga Sutras remind us that the goal of *Pranayama* is not control but consciousness. The purpose isn't to manipulate the breath. It's to meet it. When we meet our breath with awareness, we meet ourselves. In that moment, we interrupt the pattern of reactivity. Instead of snapping, we soften. Instead of unraveling, we center.

Energetic mastery doesn't mean you never get triggered. It means you recover faster. It means your body learns a new baseline. One rooted in peace instead of panic. Over time, your breath becomes the cue your nervous system trusts most.

This is especially powerful for women who grew up around anxiety, tension, or volatility. Those environments teach the body to brace for impact. Through breathwork, we teach it to rest in safety instead. We retrain our internal system to recognize calm as normal, not as a threat.

The power of breathwork extends beyond personal regulation. It's generational reprogramming. When you breathe consciously, *you're not only calming your own body; you're recalibrating your lineage.* You're teaching your children and those who witness you that peace is accessible at any moment.

Breath is life's reminder that we always have a choice. You can't always control what happens, but you can always control how you breathe through it. And that small, sacred choice changes everything.

The longer I practice, the more I understand that mastery is not about doing more; it's about returning to the simplest truths. Inhale. Exhale. Begin again. That rhythm has healed more pain than any complicated method ever could.

HOW EACH ARCHETYPE EXPERIENCES THIS

Stagnant Stella

For Stella, breathing has always been unconscious. She moves through life holding her breath, literally and emotionally. Raised in a family that equated composure with control, she learned early that emotions were inconvenient. When she feels tension, she tightens. When she feels fear, she freezes. Her shoulders rise with every worry, her chest constricts with every unspoken thought. Stella's nervous system lives on alert, constantly waiting for the next problem to solve or person to please.

Her body has forgotten what peace feels like. She often experiences fatigue, headaches, and restlessness without realizing they're symptoms of shallow breathing. For Stella, breathwork feels foreign at first. Stillness feels suspicious. But when she starts practicing slow, intentional inhales and exhales, something miraculous happens. Her tears surface. Decades of unprocessed emotion begin to melt through her breath. *With each exhale, she learns that releasing isn't weakness; it's wisdom.* Her healing begins when she stops bracing for life and starts breathing through it.

Searching Serena

Serena knows about breathwork. She's watched videos, attended workshops, even bookmarked YouTube meditations titled "Calm Your Mind Now." But she struggles with consistency. She tries square breathing one week, then ratio breathing the next, never giving herself enough time to settle into stillness. Her mind races faster than her lungs can keep up.

When life feels heavy, Serena instinctively looks outside herself for relief. She scrolls, shops, or signs up for something new. But through this search, she starts realizing that peace isn't something she can find; it's something she can create. Her journey with breath becomes one of trust. Trusting that the body knows what the mind resists.

Her turning point comes when she starts using breathwork in real time. Instead of reacting to a stressful email or heated conversation, she pauses and breathes. *That single conscious breath shifts everything.* She starts recognizing that mastery isn't about perfection; it's about presence.

Thriving Theresa

Theresa's relationship with breath is sacred. She's learned that the way she breathes is the way she lives: deeply, intentionally, and with grace. Her mornings begin with slow inhales of gratitude and long exhales of surrender. Breathwork isn't an afterthought; it's a lifestyle.

Theresa understands that energy is currency. She regulates her nervous system not exclusively for herself but for everyone she leads, mentors, and loves. *She uses breath to reset before speaking, before teaching, before making big decisions.* Her calm becomes contagious. In meetings, she breathes before responding. With family, she uses breath to soften tension. With herself, she uses it to return home.

Her mastery isn't about escaping emotion. It's about channeling it. She no longer lets her breath follow her stress; she lets her breath lead her peace. And because she breathes differently, she lives differently. Her legacy is calm.

Through these three archetypes, we see the full spectrum of inherited breath patterns, from unconscious holding to conscious release to embodied regulation. Each woman teaches us something vital: the breath you take today can rewrite generations of reactivity.

LUXE LIFESTYLE RITUAL: The Generational Reset Breath

The breath is your body's built-in reset button. It requires no equipment, no special timing, no appointment, only intention. The **Generational Reset Breath** is a practice designed to interrupt reactive cycles and restore calm to your nervous system before old patterns take over. It's short, powerful, and meant to travel with you wherever life happens.

Step 1: Prepare the Space

Find a quiet corner, or simply pause wherever you are. Rest your feet flat on the ground. Place one hand over your heart and one over your belly. Feel the weight of your body supported by the earth beneath you.

Step 2: The 4-4-4 Pattern

Inhale gently through your nose for four counts. Hold the breath softly for four counts. Exhale slowly through your mouth for four counts. Pause briefly before the next inhale.

Repeat this pattern for at least four rounds. With each breath, feel your body soften and your energy settle. This rhythm regulates both the mind and the nervous system, signaling safety to your body.

Step 3: Integrate the Intention

As you breathe, repeat silently: *"With every breath, I reset my lineage."*

Allow this affirmation to anchor your awareness. You are calming yourself. Plus you are teaching your body, your children, and your lineage a new pattern of peace.

Step 4: Use It in Real Time

Before family gatherings, difficult conversations, or moments of overwhelm, take a pause to breathe. Use this ritual as a bridge between reaction and response. It's a tool of transformation that can be practiced anytime: during your commute, in a meeting, or before bed.

Breathwork doesn't remove challenges; it reshapes how you meet them. Over time, the Generational Reset Breath becomes your new baseline. Calm replaces chaos. Presence replaces panic. Regulation replaces reactivity.

This is luxury at its deepest level: energy mastery as self-preservation.

PATTERN RECOGNITION BOX

The more I practiced conscious breathing, the more I realized it wasn't merely a relaxation tool. It was reprogramming my lineage. Breathwork became the foundation for everything else. Each inhale felt like reclaiming energy that had been trapped for generations, and each exhale felt like releasing what no longer needed to live in my body.

I began noticing how *my breath changed my choices*. The pause between inhale and exhale became the space between reaction and response. That space was sacred. It was where healing happened. The more I practiced, the more my nervous system learned a new pattern: calm was safe, stillness was productive, and peace was power.

I could feel the shift ripple through my family. My children started breathing through their challenges instead of pushing through them. Conversations softened. Energy shifted. We were rewriting our relationship with stress, one conscious breath at a time.

I understood then that changing my breath was literally changing what I would pass down. Breath wasn't entirely air. It was ancestry in motion.

LUXENARY BRIDGE: Your Next Evolution

Your transition into the next spiral point

But breath is only the beginning of your recalibration. Once you learn to regulate your energy, the next invitation is to protect it, to stop absorbing the noise, the chaos, and the inherited urgency that has kept your nervous system on alert.

In the next chapter, you'll step into **Sacred Stillness** (Pratyahara), where you learn that peace is not passive. It is a practice. It is a choice. And it is the foundation everything else is built upon.

You've learned to breathe through the storm. Now you'll learn to stop inviting it in.

REFLECTION PROMPTS (Energetic Mastery)

Use these prompts to deepen your breath-centered awakening:

1. What stress patterns or coping behaviors did you witness growing up that still live in your body today?

2. How does your breathing change in moments of conflict, pressure, or emotional overwhelm?

3. Where in your life do you hold your breath: literally or metaphorically?

4. What emotions surface when you pause long enough to breathe before reacting?

5. How has shallow breathing shaped your relationship with anxiety or control?

6. What would "breathing like a woman who feels safe" look and feel like for you?

7. How can breathwork become your go-to tool for grounding instead of your last resort?

8. Write one reminder you can use in real time: "When I breathe, I _______."

DAWNISM

"Change your breath; change your frequency."

AFFIRMATIONS

I breathe with intention, grounding myself in the present moment. I release the inherited tension my body no longer needs to hold. My breath is my power, my peace, and my protection. With every inhale and exhale, I choose regulation over reactivity.

"Stillness is intelligence, not emptiness."

DAWNISM

Dawn M. Rivers

Chapter 10

YOU WERE RAISED ON NOISE. NOW YOU HAVE TO LEARN QUIET.

nd why silence feels so uncomfortable

Maybe my mom felt trapped and was disappointed at the unmet expectations and promises my stepfather made when they first married, but she seemed angry all throughout my childhood. My stepfather was an alcoholic and a workaholic. She was introverted and didn't like attending the various functions he was invited to as the editor of the Call & Post, a leading Black newspaper. He was known all over the city and loved the attention. She did not. Because of this she was lonely.

I believe the loneliness was like a prison or a cage for her. She wanted my brother and me to be raised with two parents in the house with the trappings of a suburban neighborhood. We had all of that. We were one of the first families to have a computer game system and a second phone line in our house. We took vacations every year, went out for steak dinners every Friday, and were given an allowance. My brother and I lacked for nothing after living on food stamps, government assistance, and in low income areas.

At one point in time my mom took up gardening. She had a beautiful flower garden with flowering trees, rose bushes, a trellis and patio furniture. My stepfather had a vegetable garden. I think this was the first time that they started to connect outside of their old ways of parties and drinking. My mom had started going to church, stopped drinking, and prayed nonstop. She was believing for a miracle that her husband would be "saved" but my mom also gave him an ultimatum to stop drinking or she was going to divorce him. I think he didn't want to have another failed marriage because his two older sons suffered from the breakup. He stopped drinking. It saved their marriage.

My mom was doing all she could to turn the chaos into a cultured experience by controlling the outcome. She wanted nice things, to go to the theatre, and travel more. It was hard to convince my stepfather to work less but by this time he knew if he didn't change, she would leave.

As a child, my mom put a lock on my bedroom door. I don't remember the exact reason that predicated her actions but I think she was uncomfortable with my stepfather's behavior and wanted to make sure I was safe. It's likely that I suppressed the memories but I do remember my mom putting the lock on the door.

As a teenager. I found a job and rode my bike to work and to my friends' houses. I was involved in school activities and was in a social group. I was happy and obedient. If my curfew was before midnight, I was home on time. I did try to move the line occasionally but my mom always found out. Overall, I didn't want to do the things my friends were doing. This was my way of finding peace and control over what I could.

When I was either a sophomore or junior in high school I tried to meditate. I don't know why or remember where this thought came from but I do remember having an outer body feeling that I later learned was a transcendental experience. It was a euphoric moment and I was at peace. I never felt like this again until I was in my forties.

Decades later at a yoga conference in Toronto, I attended a breathwork session that took me on another outer body sensation that both frightened and excited me. Looking down on my body from above shocked me and I felt like I was scrambling to get back down to my body. Nevertheless, after the teacher brought us "back to ourselves," I realized I had that euphoric feeling again as I did when I was a teen. After returning home, I started to incorporate more meditative practices like this in both my personal life and with my students.

That first time as a teenager seared something in me. Looking back I know now I was forever on a quest for peace. Through the chaos in my childhood home, to the abuse in my adulthood, to rebuilding life after divorce. The search continued. Now I call it happiness, wholeness, and freedom, but at the core was always peace that I was searching.

THE INHERITED BLUEPRINT: The Generational Fear of Slowing Down

In many families, chaos is the soundtrack of survival. It's the unspoken rhythm that fills the silence, a familiar hum that convinces us we're safe as long as something is happening. When I look back, I see that my family didn't live in chaos when I was a child; we became fluent in it. It was our language, our coping mechanism, and our identity.

My mother's version of control was her way of managing the noise that lived inside her. She tried to curate peace through perfection, protection, and prayer, but I believe stillness frightened her. Silence felt uncertain, and uncertainty felt unsafe. She believed that if she could just keep everything and everyone in line, she could hold chaos at bay. My stepfather coped differently. His busyness, love of work, and constant motion were ways of avoiding stillness too. It's no wonder that as a child, I equated quiet with tension.

This is how the pattern of overstimulation is passed down, not always through shouting or conflict, but through a nervous system that never rests. Children raised in chaos often become adults who *confuse calm with boredom*. The mind starts to believe that movement equals meaning, and rest equals risk. Even joy can feel uncomfortable when you've inherited a body trained to anticipate the next crisis.

As women, we often become the peacekeepers in our families, yet we forget to keep peace within ourselves. We pour our energy into diffusing drama, managing relationships, and maintaining appearances. But when the noise stops, we feel exposed, vulnerable, even lost. That's when the deeper truth emerges. We were never afraid of silence itself; we were afraid of what it might reveal.

Breaking this generational pattern means redefining what peace feels like. It's not the absence of responsibility or sound; it's the recalibration of energy. **Sacred stillness** teaches us that the quiet we once feared is actually where healing begins. It's where intuition speaks, where nervous systems repair, and where lineage learns to rest.

Every time we choose stillness over stimulation, we break a cycle. We tell our bodies, "It's safe to slow down." We tell our ancestors, "The fight is over." And we tell our descendants, "Peace is your birthright."

What Pratyahara Taught Me About Choosing Peace

Stillness is not about isolation. It's about integration. It's the spiritual exhale that allows the body, mind, and soul to realign after generations of overextension. In the philosophy of yoga, *Pratyahara* means "the withdrawal of the senses." But withdrawal doesn't mean escape. It means consciously turning your attention inward to restore balance, awareness, and inner harmony.

For generations, especially in families shaped by struggle or survival, the ability to rest was seen as indulgent. Stillness was often associated with laziness, avoidance, or weakness. The unspoken rule was: *keep moving, keep fixing, keep proving.* And so we did, until we forgot how to be still at all.

This overidentification with doing is part of the inheritance many women carry. We overcommit, overfunction, and overstimulate ourselves, believing that constant motion keeps us safe from the chaos we grew up in. We fill every quiet space with conversation, noise, and activity because silence feels foreign. The nervous system interprets calm as danger when chaos was once comfort.

Pratyahara invites us to reverse that conditioning. It teaches us to disconnect from external noise, not to ignore life, but to reclaim our energy from it. By softening sensory input, we create space for inner wisdom to rise. In a world obsessed with visibility, stillness becomes a quiet revolution.

This practice isn't only about meditating in silence or sitting in a dark room, but it is also about choosing what enters your energy field. It's turning down the volume on everyone else's expectations so you can finally hear your own intuition. It's closing your eyes not to escape reality but to see it more clearly.

In my own life, the deeper I practiced stillness, the more I realized how overstimulated I had been. Even the noble things—helping, teaching, creating—could become noise when done without intention. I began to understand that sacred stillness wasn't about removing life; it was about refining it. It's the art of knowing when to engage and when to retreat, when to speak and when to listen, when to act and when to rest.

In the Yoga Sutras, *Pratyahara* acts as a bridge between the external practices of discipline and the internal practices of awareness. It's the moment we begin to reclaim authority over our attention. When we withdraw from the external world, we can finally observe the inner one with clarity.

Energetically, this is where generational healing deepens. When we stop reacting to every stimulus—every text, every family crisis, every emotional demand—we begin to regulate the energy that once ruled us. The noise fades, and truth rises.

Stillness doesn't mean disengagement; it means discernment. It allows you to show up with presence instead of performance. It teaches you that not every battle needs your sword, and not every cry requires your rescue. Sometimes, the most powerful response is the pause.

Through stillness, we rewire our lineage's nervous system. We send a new message through the bloodline: *Peace is not passive. It is power contained.*

That's the essence of *Pratyahara*. The practice of choosing peace as your new pattern, not because life has quieted, but because you have.

HOW EACH ARCHETYPE EXPERIENCES THIS

Stagnant Stella

For Stella, silence feels threatening. She grew up in a home where noise meant safety, and stillness signaled danger. She learned early to stay busy. Talking, working, or cleaning filled the silence that might expose pain. When she finally slows down, the quiet is deafening. Every suppressed thought, every unprocessed feeling rushes to the surface. Stillness feels like confrontation.

Stella's nervous system doesn't yet trust rest. She fills her downtime with scrolling, talking, or "doing something productive." If she stops, she fears she'll lose control. Her journey begins when she starts noticing how overstimulation drains her energy and how quiet moments trigger old survival responses.

Her breakthrough comes when she learns to sit in the discomfort without rushing to fix it. The first time she allows herself to rest without guilt, to breathe without distraction, she realizes that the world doesn't collapse when she pauses. That moment becomes her portal to peace.

Searching Serena

Serena wants calm desperately. She listens to guided meditations, buys noise-canceling headphones, and journals about peace, but her mind races even in silence. Her restlessness isn't a lack of effort; it's the residue of inherited chaos. She's used to equating productivity with worth. When she's still, guilt whispers that she should be doing more.

Serena's path toward sacred stillness begins with permission. Permission to log off, to say no, to sit with herself without needing a plan. In the beginning, she mistakes quiet for boredom, but over time she learns that boredom is one of the ways the body transitions into rest.

One evening, she lights a candle, closes her laptop, and simply sits. Her mind protests at first, but then, something shifts. In the soft hum of her breath, she hears her own wisdom rising. The chaos isn't gone, but it no longer owns her. *Serena discovers that stillness isn't the absence of noise; it's the awareness beneath it.*

Thriving Theresa

Theresa lives by the truth that stillness is strategy. She no longer views silence as luxury; she sees it as leadership. Her mornings begin in solitude. There are no screens, no sound, only the sacred symphony of her own breath. Stillness is her meeting place with God, her boardroom for divine downloads.

She's learned that protecting her peace doesn't require explanation. She no longer feels obligated to attend every family event or answer every phone call. Her boundaries aren't walls; they're invitations for others to rise in emotional maturity. When chaos calls, she doesn't pick up—she prays, breathes, and listens.

Through practice, *Theresa has become the calm in her family's storm.* Her presence de-escalates tension. Her peace feels like protection. The same silence that once felt foreign now feels familiar, a sanctuary she built from within.

Each archetype's relationship to stillness reveals a stage of transformation: resistance, practice, and embodiment. The evolution from chaos to calm isn't instant; it's intentional. Every woman must unlearn her family's definition of peace before she can create her own.

Stillness isn't about escaping the world; it's about engaging it from wholeness. When we withdraw from noise, we don't lose connection. We deepen it. This is the quiet revolution of the Spiral Path: healing not through more doing, but through sacred being.

LUXE LIFESTYLE RITUAL: The Family Boundary Practice

Sacred stillness isn't something you stumble into; it's something you curate. It's not about waiting for peace to appear but creating environments that invite it. The *Family Boundary Practice* is your energetic declaration that you will no longer participate in inherited chaos. It's how you transform peace from a passing moment into a lifestyle.

Step 1: Begin with a Digital Sunset

Each evening, choose a time, preferably an hour before bed, to turn off devices. No news, no notifications, no noise. This signals to your nervous system that you are no longer available for the world's chaos. Light a candle, stretch gently, or sip herbal tea as your body transitions into calm. This nightly ritual is your cue to withdraw from sensory stimulation and return to self.

Step 2: Energy Protection Before Family Interactions

Before visiting family, taking a call, or entering any emotionally charged space, pause. Place one hand on your heart and the other on your solar plexus. Take three slow breaths, saying quietly:

"My peace is my protection. My energy is my boundary." This practice trains your nervous system to remain grounded, even in environments where others may still be operating in chaos. You're not detaching from love; you're detaching from dysfunction.

Step 3: Create Sacred Space Within Chaos

You can't always control your surroundings, but you can design micro-moments of serenity. Create an altar or small sacred corner at home with objects that represent calm: a photo, a plant, a candle, or a crystal. When family tension rises, retreat to that space for five minutes. Breathe. Listen inwardly. Stillness becomes your sanctuary, not the reward after exhaustion.

Step 4: Practice the Stillness Sequence

This can be done sitting, standing, or lying down. Close your eyes, inhale for four counts, hold for four, exhale for four, and hold again for four. (*Box breathing*). Do this three times while silently repeating, "I am safe in my stillness." You are literally rewiring the generational imprint that associates silence with danger.

Over time, this ritual becomes more than a practice. It becomes an identity. You start to respond instead of react, to listen instead of absorb, to protect instead of perform. The peace you create ripples backward through your lineage and forward into your legacy.

Because when a woman learns to rest in her own stillness, she is not only changes her own life; she rewrites her family's energetic story.

PATTERN RECOGNITION BOX

Stillness became the thread that wove all my practices together. What began as a simple act of breathing and unplugging turned into a profound revelation: every generational pattern I was breaking required silence first.

When I stopped reacting to family chaos, I started noticing the rhythm beneath it. The cycle of overextension, exhaustion, and emotional collapse that had repeated for decades. My mother filled the silence with prayer and control. I filled it with productivity and purpose. Different behaviors, same energy: constant motion.

The first time I chose stillness instead of strategy, something shifted. I heard my own thoughts before they turned into overreactions. I felt the ancestral noise start to dissolve in the quiet. What had once felt like emptiness began to feel like expansion.

That's when I understood that stillness is not the absence of action; it's the foundation of aligned action. It's where clarity lives.

My son was having a difficult time with his dad during his visit home for Christmas. My son needed to be reminded that he was an adult and allowed to set up a boundary with his dad. I gave him a simple framework of "if, then." For example, you tell the person if you do X, then I will do Y. If you yell, belittle, or insult me, than I will end the conversation, leave, or not continue to interact with you until you sincerely apologize and prove that your behavior has changed.

This was the moment I could see the Spiral Pattern forming; the same one I had witnessed in my clients, students, and archetypes. Every woman seeking healing moves through this same sequence: from chaos to clarity, from reaction to response, from inherited noise to intentional peace.

Stillness wasn't the end of the work; it was the sacred beginning of it all.

LUXENARY BRIDGE: Your Next Evolution

Your transition into the next spiral point

Sacred Stillness is the moment a woman stops performing for the world and starts listening to herself. It's where she stops absorbing generational noise and begins hearing her own truth. But stillness is only one gate in your evolution. Once you learn to quiet the chaos within and around you, a new dimension of clarity opens, the kind that prepares you for deeper focus, embodied intuition, and unwavering presence.

In the next chapter, you'll step into **Dharana**, the Spiral Point of focused intention. It's where your calm becomes concentration, your awareness becomes direction, and your peace becomes power.

REFLECTION PROMPTS (Sacred Stillness)

Use these prompts to deepen your Sacred Stillness practice:

1. What chaos patterns did you inherit from your family, and how have they shaped your relationship with rest?

2. When was the last time you allowed yourself to sit in silence without performing, pleasing, or producing?

3. How does your body respond when you try to be still, and what might that reveal about your nervous system's history?

4. What forms of stimulation (scrolling, noise, problem-solving) do you use to avoid your own inner world?

5. Whose expectations or emergencies still pull you out of your peace?

6. What small, sacred space can you create to honor your stillness, even for five minutes a day?

7. Which relationships require energetic boundaries before you can truly rest?

8. How might your life shift if you treated stillness as a non-negotiable instead of a reward?

DAWNISM

"Stillness is intelligence, not emptiness."

AFFIRMATIONS

I choose peace over performance. I release the chaos I inherited and return to myself with clarity. My stillness is powerful, protective, and sacred. Every quiet breath rewrites my lineage and restores my spirit.

> *Whatever you place your attention on becomes your future.*

DAWNISM
Dawn M. Rivers

Chapter 11

YOU CAN'T DRIVE FORWARD LOOKING IN THE REARVIEW MIRROR

Your Ancestors Survived Day to Day. You Get to Build a Future.

When my older brother was 16, he and a friend were speeding while driving my mom's car and drove into a tree. He hit his head on the windshield but overall was okay. My mother wasn't and her fear was projected on me. I was not allowed to get my drivers license even though I had completed and passed my driving school classes and the test. This fear didn't come through as concern but as control. She ruled with a strict and stern hand. I didn't feel as my opinions were being heard or understood.

As a senior in high school my curfew was 11 pm and I didn't push the limits. I can only remember two times I was sneaky and didn't tell my mom the truth about my whereabouts. One was with my social group, Savior Faire. We were at a hotel with a bunch of guys playing games, dancing, and having an honest good time. But things went south quickly because the boys began to horseplay and broke a window. Somehow my mom found out about it and I'm pretty sure I was grounded for it. The other time I said I was sleeping over at my friend's house, but we went to a party instead of staying home. My friends and I were going to be drinking and dancing when my mom came downstairs to where the party was and took me home. I was mortified but didn't push the limits again.

When I became a parent I tried my best to keep my own experiences in mind, let my children have a say in what they wanted, while keeping guardrails around them. Believe me, I made my share of mistakes as a parent and was sometimes distracted by my marriage, but overall I think they felt as if they had freedom of choice.

I know my mother wanted more for me and she was afraid of me experiencing things that were prevalent in the 1980s: sex, drugs, pregnancy, and alcohol. Unfortunately, I was sheltered and not fully prepared to be a young adult in college and made poor choices once I left home.

When I went to college I had no direction and eventually came home as a single mother. When my daughter was two years old, I knew I wanted more for her. I started to plan for our lives. I was going to get my masters degree, become a librarian and move to Chicago with my good friend after she graduated from college. This was one of my favorite places and my dad lived there. I had envisioned myself working at the Chicago Public Library's downtown main branch. My friend would be a teacher and she would help me raise Brittany as her godmother.

Then plans changed. I got married and soon became librarian in my childhood neighborhood library. One day, a middle school student came in to get books for a research project. Her sixth-grade class was going to Cape Cod to study their ecosystem. I was astounded. This little Black girl who loved science was going to study seagrass up in Maine for a week. At that moment I decided that Brittany would attend this same all girls school. It was exclusive and expensive, but I didn't care about that. Nine years later, she went on that same trip and graduated from the school. My son, Brenton even went to an all boys school for two years. He graduated from public school because it was a better fit for him. He asked to return to the district where his friends were. As much as I wanted him to stay, we talked through his decision, and I honored his wishes.

THE INHERITED BLUEPRINT: The Generational Habit of Dreaming Small

For many families, especially those shaped by scarcity, struggle, or survival, the future was never a place you planned for. It was a place you hoped you reached. When every day demanded your full attention to make it through, vision wasn't practical. It was a luxury you hadn't earned. And so, generation after generation, the ability to imagine a life beyond the immediate was quietly discouraged, not out of cruelty, but out of protection.

My mother's worldview was shaped by what she had witnessed and survived.

She kept my brother and me close, monitored, and contained. When I wanted to go to Mexico on a school exchange program, she said no. Not because she didn't love me, but because she couldn't see past the fear. Her fear was founded. She had lived through an era when Black students who dared to step outside the lines of what was expected of them were arrested, harassed, and worse. She was protecting me from a world she knew. What she didn't know was that the world had shifted, and her protection had become a ceiling.

I didn't get my driver's license when I was supposed to. I didn't study abroad in college. I didn't know that was even a possibility for someone like me. That's the quiet damage of "that's not for us" thinking. It doesn't always announce itself as limitation. It shows up as common sense. As practicality. As love.

What I now understand is that my mother wasn't dreaming small on purpose. She was dreaming at the edge of what she could see. Many of her ancestors had survived day to day with no permission, no invitation, and no margin to envision anything beyond the present moment. She had some relatives who left her family compound, but they still faced tremendous hardships.

You don't build a ten-year plan when you're not sure about tomorrow. That survival instinct was passed down through the bloodline as wisdom. Stay close. Don't reach too far. Know your place before someone reminds you of it.

By the time that inheritance reached me, it felt like personality. I went to college with no direction because no one in my immediate world had given me a map. My mother said that I had to go to college. This was the way Americans succeeded, especially if you were Black.

But I drifted. I came home. I started over. It wasn't laziness. It was the result of never having been invited to imagine my own future.

The turning point came in a library. Not mine, someone else's. When that middle school girl walked in to prepare for a research trip to Cape Cod. She was small, Black, focused, and completely unafraid of her own possibility. Something in me cracked open watching her. I thought: *Brittany will go to this school.* I didn't ask whether it was realistic. I didn't calculate the cost first. I made the decision and Brittany went to that same all girls school.

That moment taught me something the inheritance never had: vision is a practice. It requires you to see something before it exists. To hold it steady long enough for the world to catch up.

The Brazil trip deepened that lesson. I didn't leave my selection to chance. I told the program coordinators I wanted to go to Brazil. I said it directly. I wrote about it. I made the case. When they announced the assignments, they sent me to Brazil because I had claimed it. I didn't wait to be chosen. I chose myself first.

That is what scarcity thinking steals from us. Not only opportunity, but the audacity to pursue it. When survival is the family operating system, desire feels dangerous. Wanting more than what your mother had can feel like betrayal. Naming a vision out loud can feel foolish when no one around you has ever dared to do the same.

But your ancestors didn't endure what they endured so you could stay where they were forced to stop. They survived so you could finally look up. The dreaming they never got to do belongs to you now. And holding a vision long enough to live inside it, that is not indulgence. That is inheritance reclaimed.

Dharana Is Why I Could Finally See My Future

For most of my life, I didn't have a vision. I had reactions. I moved from one decision to the next based on what was happening around me rather than what I was building toward. That's what generational survival does, it trains you to manage the present moment so completely that the future never becomes real. You can't plan what you can't imagine. And when your family has been in crisis mode for generations, imagination feels like a luxury you haven't earned.

In yoga philosophy, *Dharana* means concentrated focus: the deliberate practice of holding a single point of awareness without distraction. It is the sixth limb of yoga, and it is often translated as "single-pointed concentration." The Yoga Sutras teach that the undisciplined mind scatters its energy across a thousand directions at once. Dharana is the practice of gathering that energy back and directing it with intention toward one thing.

When I first encountered this teaching, I recognized myself in its opposite. My attention had been fragmented my entire life. I was watching for danger, managing my mother's emotions, compensating for my stepfather's absences, and responding to whatever needed handling in the moment. I was reactive, not visionary. My nervous system was tuned to crisis, not creation.

Our ancestors survived by staying alert to immediate threats. That hypervigilance kept them alive. But it also kept their eyes locked on what was directly in front of them, not what was ten years ahead. When survival is the operating system, the future isn't a destination. It's a threat.

Dharana breaks that pattern. It asks you to do something radical: choose one vision and hold it steady, even when everything around you is pulling at your attention. It trains the mind to stay, to resist the inherited urgency that says, *look over there, fix this first, handle that before you can rest.* It asks you to trust that holding your focus is itself an act of healing.

When I finally allowed myself to envision a future — truly picture it, feel it, speak it out loud — something shifted in my body. I remember the moment I stood in that public library and looked at that little Black girl heading to Cape Cod for science research. I held that image in my mind like a prayer and I didn't let it go.

That is Dharana in action. Not wishful thinking. Not a vision board you forget about in February. Concentrated, unwavering, devotional focus on a future you have chosen to create.

Your lineage may have survived day to day. You get to plan a decade at a time.

HOW EACH ARCHETYPE EXPERIENCES THIS

Stagnant Stella

Stella has never been given permission to have a vision. Every time she began to imagine a different life, someone needed something, a crisis arose, or her own inner voice reminded her that wanting more was dangerous or selfish. Her focus has always been outward: managing, maintaining, surviving. When she tries to sit with a single desire or goal, her mind immediately floods with reasons it won't work, problems that need solving first, and guilt about dreaming at all.

For Stella, Dharana begins with the smallest possible act of focus. Not a five-year plan, a single sentence: *what do I want?* She has been so occupied with everyone else's needs that she has lost the thread of her own desire. Her first practice is simply to ask the question and sit with it long enough to hear an answer. When she writes down one vision and returns to it daily, something ancient begins to stir.

She discovers that her ancestors didn't endure so she could stay small. They endured so she could finally look up.

Searching Serena

Serena doesn't have a vision; she has seventeen of them. Her problem is not imagination, it is concentration. She generates ideas constantly and chases each one with genuine excitement until the next arrives and pulls her in a different direction. Her scattered focus isn't laziness; it's inherited urgency dressed up as ambition. She moves fast because stillness feels like falling behind.

Dharana is the practice Serena needs most and resists most deeply. When she finally commits to one vision and holds it, when she stops adding to the list and starts deepening her relationship with a single intention, everything changes. She discovers that focus is not a cage. It is a filter. It shows her which opportunities belong to her vision and which ones are simply noise. Her mantra becomes: *I do not chase every open door. I trust the one that feels like home.*

Thriving Theresa

Theresa has learned to live from vision rather than reaction. She wakes each morning with intention, not urgency. She has trained her mind through years of practice to hold her focus steady even when the world around her is demanding her attention. Dharana is not a new concept for her; it is the invisible architecture of her daily life.

What Theresa now understands is that her concentrated focus is a generational gift. Every time she holds her vision steady instead of scattering her energy in response to family chaos or external pressure, she is modeling something her lineage has never seen before: a woman who knows where she is going and refuses to be pulled off course. Her children watch her. Her nieces watch her. Her community watches her. And what they see is proof that clarity is possible, that the future is plannable, and that a woman who knows her direction changes the direction of everyone who comes after her.

Through Stella, Serena, and Theresa, we see the evolution of vision focus: from scarcity to clarity, from inherited limitation to devoted intention. Each woman represents a stage of returning home to herself. When we withdraw from the noise of the world, we don't lose connection. We deepen it.

Stillness becomes the portal to clarity, and clarity becomes the foundation of freedom.

LUXE LIFESTYLE RITUAL: The Generational Vision Focus Practice

A ritual for clarity, direction, and breaking the lineage of distraction

Your ancestors survived without the luxury of long-term vision. Many lived day-to-day, crisis-to-crisis, doing the best they could without the space to dream beyond necessity.

You are the first woman in your lineage with the privilege, and responsibility to focus.

This ritual helps you practice Dharana by training your mind to hold your intention long enough for it to become reality.

Step 1: Clear the Mental Field (2 minutes)

- Before you focus, you must release. Sit quietly, close your eyes, and take three slow breaths. Imagine wiping dust off a glass window. That window is your mind.

- Repeat softly: **"I release what is not mine to carry."**

- This clears inherited mental clutter and prepares your mind for clarity.

Step 2: Choose One Single Desire (Not a To-Do List)

- Dharana is not multitasking. It is devotion.

- Ask yourself: **"What is the one thing I want my future self to thank me for?"**

- Write down one desire, vision, or goal. Not ten. Just one.

- This breaks the generational pattern of scattered attention and survival mode action.

Step 3: Create a Focus Container (5 minutes)

- Choose a physical object that symbolizes your vision: a candle, stone, necklace, journal, or photo. This becomes your **Focus Anchor**.

- Hold it. Breathe with it. Let your nervous system connect the object to the vision.

- Your body will recognize it faster than your mind.

Step 4: Hold the Vision for 90 Seconds

- This is the heart of Dharana.

  - Set a timer.

  - Close your eyes.

  - See the vision.

  - Feel it.

- ○ Stay with it.

- Any mind wandering is normal, gently return to the vision without judgment.

- You are strengthening the part of your brain responsible for discipline, manifestation, and long-term decision-making.

Step 5: Take One Micro Action (3 minutes)

- Ask: *"What is one next step the woman in this vision would take today?"*

- Then take that step immediately. Not the biggest step. The truest one.

- This rewrites the lineage of procrastination, chaos, and emotional numbing with clarity, momentum, and trust.

Why This Ritual Matters

Practiced consistently, the *Generational Vision Focus Ritual* becomes a spiritual discipline that awakens your inner leader. It breaks inherited patterns of fear, distraction, and pressure; replacing them with clarity, confidence, and purpose.

Vision becomes your compass. Focus becomes your frequency. Your life rises to match the woman you are becoming.

PATTERN RECOGNITION BOX

The more I practiced Dharana, the more I noticed what happened when I stopped letting everything compete for my attention. For most of my life I believed I was unfocused because something was wrong with me. What I discovered was that scattered attention is inherited. When survival is the operating system, the mind learns to watch everything at once. Hypervigilance isn't a personality trait. It's a nervous system strategy. And it follows you into adulthood disguised as ambition, busyness, or an inability to finish what you start.

The pattern I kept seeing in myself and in my clients was this: we could dream, but we couldn't hold the dream. We would get excited, lose momentum, and conclude we weren't disciplined enough. But it wasn't discipline we were missing. It was permission. The deep cellular belief that a woman like us was allowed to want one thing and stay with it long enough for it to become real.

Dharana broke that open for me. Not because it gave me a new goal, but because it gave me a new relationship with my own attention. The moment I stopped treating focus as a willpower problem and started treating it as a healing practice, everything shifted. I began to trust my vision instead of abandoning it every time life got loud.

That's the spiral pattern with Dharana: you don't chase focus. You heal your way into it.

LUXENARY BRIDGE: Your Next Evolution

Vision Focus is where your transformation sharpens. After stillness teaches you to quiet the noise, Dharana teaches you to direct your energy with clarity and intention. This is the moment you stop drifting and start deciding.

You've explored your patterns, reconnected with your inner truth, and begun practicing sacred stillness. Now you step into the spiral point where focus becomes a spiritual strategy. The woman you are becoming doesn't limit herself to a dream. She concentrates her power, aligns her attention, and chooses what her lineage couldn't imagine.

In the next chapter, you'll move into **Presence Embodiment**, where focus becomes devotion and your identity begins to match your destiny.

Your evolution is accelerating and your clarity is leading the way.

REFLECTION PROMPTS (Vision Focus)

Use these prompts to deepen your work with Dharana:

1. What limiting beliefs about success or possibilities did you inherit from your family?

2. Where does your attention naturally go: chaos or clarity?

3. What dreams feel "too big," and who taught you to think that way?

4. Which distractions most often pull you out of alignment?

5. When do you feel the clearest sense of purpose?

6. What vision keeps returning to you no matter how much you try to ignore it?

7. What would happen if you allowed yourself to want what you truly want?

8. What is one bold, focused decision you can make this week that honors your highest self?

DAWNISM

"Whatever you place your attention on becomes your future."

AFFIRMATIONS

I choose clarity over confusion. I focus my energy on what expands me. I honor the visions that rise from my soul. I am committed, grounded, and aligned with my next level.

> # *Presence is the ultimate luxury.*

DAWNISM

Dawn M. Rivers

Chapter 12
YOU'VE BEEN SHOWING UP. NOW TRY ACTUALLY ARRIVING.

resence requires more than participation

Years after my mother had her stroke, she pulled more and more away from me even though I lived with her. She barely spoke to me. She didn't want to leave the house, not for doctor's appointments, not for events, not even to get her hair cut. It was exhausting and extremely difficult to live with someone who had given up on life and refused to take antidepressants.

Doctors, therapists, social workers, family and friends all tried to intervene with no success. Because she was cognizant, there wasn't anything I could do to prevent her suffering and downward decline.

She could "care" for herself.
She took her medication and answered all the questions of the visiting nurses.
She was conscious in body but her mind wanted to be on the other side.

For close to a decade, my mother often said she "just wanted to die." It made me angry and resentful. She didn't see how much it affected me or her grandchildren. Day by sad day, she became more reclusive and only talked to me if she needed me to do something for her like mail a bill, put a check in the bank, or send an email. Our relationship had dissipated.

When she was in the hospital for heart trouble and eventually diagnosed with heart failure, I implored her to go into an assisted living facility so she could get the care she needed. The caseworker and attending physician also talked her about it being the safest option for her but she didn't want to go and we had to back off.

My daughter came home to talk to my mom about the situation and see if she could convince her. And for a while my mom conceded. We were relieved. I visited a few places and set up lunch meetings for her to visit, but my mom refused to go. Then she finally said she wanted to go to a specific facility. Finally! I set up an appointment for the caseworker to come. They had a great program and my mom liked it. But when it was time for the nurses to do their assessments, my mom said she no longer wanted to proceed and asked me to cancel the appointments.

At that point I couldn't do this anymore. I had tried everything I could think of to help. On my days off working as a flight attendant, I visited several assisted living facilities, took her to appointments, and either emailed or spoke with directors, liaisons, social workers, and nurses.

I was exhausted and suffering myself. I experienced bouts of vertigo both at home and while on a trip. My blood pressure was low and I started to experience other symptoms. My doctors asked me if I was under pressure and stress. I told them I was caring for my elderly mother and had been trying to get her to move into an assisted living facility for over a year.

One doctor told me what we flight attendants tell our passengers: put your oxygen mask on first before assisting others.

This was a wake up call for me. I couldn't make my mom do anything. She had lived her life. She wanted to live her remaining years, no matter what the quality, in the house her husband bought for her. I conceded and accepted her wishes.

Everything shifted for me after that. I released control. I let go of trying to make things happen. I stepped back and let it be. I began to return to my grounded presence instead of the frantic overfunctioning. Peace had returned to me. Pressure had dissipated. And parenting a parent was no longer my priority.

THE INHERITED BLUEPRINT: The Lineage of Disconnection from the Self

Disconnection often masquerades as strength. In many families, especially in Black households where survival was the priority, emotional stillness and self-containment became coping mechanisms. To feel too deeply was risky. To be too aware was inconvenient. And so, generation after generation, women learned to function while detached from their own feelings, believing that endurance was the same as peace.

My mother's disconnection wasn't born from apathy; it was a form of self-protection. Life had hardened her heart because of disappointment, illness, and loss. She built walls not out of cruelty, but out of exhaustion. Her stillness was not the sacred kind; it was the silence of someone who had stopped believing that presence could change anything.

Many of us inherit that same emotional armor. We keep busy, overextend, or numb out, not because we don't care, but because presence feels dangerous. To be fully present means to witness pain, our own and others'. It means noticing where we still carry grief that isn't ours. It means sitting in rooms where the energy feels heavy and choosing not to absorb it. That level of awareness takes courage.

Generationally, disconnection becomes a survival pattern that tells us we're safer when we're distracted. Phones, streaming, work, and endless scrolling have simply modernized the behavior. What used to be cigarettes or gossip is now screen time and multitasking. The nervous system is still running from the same thing: the fear of feeling.

Breaking that cycle requires learning how to stay. Presence is not passive. It's participation with life. It's choosing to inhabit your body, your breath, your now. When we practice being present, we dismantle inherited patterns of avoidance. We teach our lineage that peace doesn't require withdrawal from the world, but engagement with it.

Meditation becomes more than a practice; it's a reclamation. When we sit in awareness, we repair the connection between mind and body, mother and daughter, past and present. We begin to experience what generations before us could not: calm without collapse, awareness without anxiety, silence without sorrow.

Every moment you choose presence, you rewrite the code. You teach your family line that safety can coexist with stillness, and that consciousness, not control, is the true inheritance of freedom.

Dhyana Taught Me What Presence Actually Feels Like

Meditation, or *Dhyana*, is the art of being here, fully, consciously, and compassionately. It isn't about escaping life; it's about meeting it without flinching. In yoga philosophy, *Dhyana* is described as the uninterrupted flow of awareness, a moment when the observer and the experience become one. But in the modern world, presence feels like a luxury most women can't afford.

For generations, we've been conditioned to equate worth with doing. Stillness was for the privileged. Rest was earned, not embodied. Our mothers and grandmothers rarely had the space to "be." They were taught that productivity was survival, and stillness was wasteful. But when the body never rests and the mind never quiets, disconnection takes root. Meditation heals this fracture by returning us to ourselves.

When I first began teaching meditation, women often confessed they couldn't "do it right." They'd say, "My mind won't stop," or "I can't sit still." I would smile and remind them: that's the practice. Presence isn't about silence in the mind; it's about awareness of what the mind is saying. We're not trying to control thoughts; we're learning to witness them without judgment.

Meditation is the antidote to inherited chaos. It invites the nervous system to exhale generations of vigilance. It teaches the body that safety can exist without control. When practiced consistently, it rewires the brain to respond rather than react. You begin to notice when old patterns arise: the urge to fix, to flee, to over-function. And instead of collapsing into them, you breathe. You stay.

Presence also changes relationships. When you learn to sit with yourself, you stop abandoning yourself in conflict. You listen differently to others and to your intuition. You realize that every person who triggers you is offering an invitation to practice consciousness. Every pause, every deep breath, becomes a portal to transformation.

This work is sacred because it reclaims something stolen: your ability to be fully alive in the moment you're living. Meditation teaches you to witness life without judgment and to choose peace over performance. It brings your awareness home to the body, where truth lives.

In generational healing, this practice becomes revolutionary. Our mothers prayed for peace but rarely experienced it. Our grandmothers held faith but carried fear in their bones. Through meditation, we become the bridge. They dreamed of rest, and we embody it.

Each inhale becomes an act of remembrance. Each exhale, a release of inherited tension. You begin to sense that your breath carries not only oxygen but wisdom. The same breath that sustained your ancestors sustains you. And when you breathe with awareness, you're healing yourself and those in our family line.

Presence isn't about perfection; it's about participation. It's showing up for your own life, moment by moment, with grace. When you practice meditation as a way of living, you are beginning to experience true embodiment. Your body becomes a sanctuary, your awareness the altar.

That's when you realize: meditation was never about quieting your mind. It was about remembering your wholeness.

HOW EACH ARCHETYPE EXPERIENCES THIS

Stagnant Stella

For Stagnant Stella, presence feels impossible. Her body may be still, but her mind is a storm. She's been raised in a household where busyness equals value, so the idea of sitting in silence makes her uneasy. When she tries to meditate, her thoughts race through to-do lists, regrets, and worries. The stillness she seeks quickly turns into discomfort.

She was taught to survive, not to *be*. Stillness reminds her of moments she couldn't control, so she fills her life with noise: TV in the background, constant scrolling, endless helping. Her nervous system is overworked, but she calls it normal. When someone tells her to just breathe, she wants to scream because no one ever taught her how.

For Stella, the path to presence begins with permission. Permission to pause, to feel, to notice. At first, a single minute of awareness feels like rebellion. But over time, she realizes that quiet doesn't equal danger; it equals healing. The first time she sits in stillness without trying to fix anything, tears come. She finally hears her own voice under all the noise.

Searching Serena

Serena has read the books, downloaded the apps, and bought the meditation cushion. She's fascinated by presence but struggles with consistency. One week she's journaling and meditating every morning; the next she's lost in distraction. She craves connection but often seeks it through information rather than embodiment.

Serena's challenge is trusting that presence doesn't need to be perfect. She's still deprogramming the belief that success, even in spirituality, comes through doing more. When she sits to meditate, she wonders if she's "doing it right." But the truth is, meditation meets her where she is.

As she practices awareness, Serena begins to notice small shifts: the way her breath slows when she walks, how her intuition whispers before she reacts. She learns that presence isn't a destination; it's a rhythm. Some days it's deep and steady; other days it's fleeting. Her transformation begins when she stops chasing peace and starts allowing it.

Through meditation, she learns to trust herself again. She stops searching for validation and starts listening inward. Presence teaches her that she's not behind. She's unfolding.

Thriving Theresa

For Thriving Theresa, presence has become her power. She's learned that grounded awareness is what keeps her balanced amid success, relationships, and leadership. Meditation is no longer a separate practice; it's woven into the way she moves through life. She cooks with presence, works with presence, listens with presence.

Theresa embodies a quiet confidence that comes from being anchored in awareness. She knows when her energy shifts and adjusts before burnout. She no longer feels the need to over-explain, over-give, or over-perform. Her peace speaks for her.

But even Thriving Theresa must remain mindful. Growth invites new challenges, and presence must deepen with each evolution. When old patterns of control or anxiety arise, she returns to the breath, not to escape, but to expand. She understands that meditation isn't about mastering stillness; it's about remembering that she *is* stillness.

Theresa models for her lineage what emotional regulation looks like in motion. Her family sees her calm in moments that would have once sparked chaos, and something subtle shifts in them too. Her presence becomes permission. Her peace becomes a generational inheritance.

LUXE LIFESTYLE RITUAL: The Conscious Presence Practice

Presence is the new luxury. It's the rarest energy in a world addicted to distraction. This ritual helps you return to yourself by cultivating conscious presence throughout your day.

Step 1: The Pause Portal

Throughout your day, notice the moments that ask for a pause, before you check your phone, respond to a message, or walk into a meeting. These micro-moments are doorways into presence. Take one deep breath in through the nose, one slow exhale through the mouth. Feel the air move through your body. You've reset your energy field.

Step 2: The Sensory Scan

Bring awareness to your senses one by one. What do you hear, smell, see, and feel? Don't label or judge, just notice. This simple practice reawakens your consciousness and pulls you out of autopilot. When practiced daily, it rewires your brain for awareness instead of anxiety.

Step 3: The Mirror Meditation

Each morning or evening, look into your own eyes in the mirror for one minute. Breathe deeply. This is not only about affirmations, but also connection. Notice what emotions arise when you hold your own gaze. You are witnessing your own presence. You are no longer abandoning yourself.

Step 4: The Anchor Affirmation

When life gets loud, whisper to yourself: *"I am here now."* Repeat until you feel the words in your body. Let your shoulders drop, your jaw soften, your heart open. This phrase becomes your internal grounding cord; your energetic reminder that you are safe in this moment.

Step 5: The Evening Integration

Before bed, take three slow breaths and reflect: *Where was I most present today? Where did I drift?* There's no shame in drifting. It's human. But by noticing, you train your awareness to return faster each time.

Presence is not about perfection; it's about participation. It's choosing to live awake rather than asleep. Every time you come back to yourself, you model a new pattern for your lineage, one of calm, clarity, and conscious living.

Presence becomes your perfume: subtle, grounding, unforgettable.

PATTERN RECOGNITION BOX

The more I practiced presence, the more I noticed how absent I had been. From conversations or moments, and from myself. I began to see how often women, especially those carrying generations of responsibility, live in a constant state of partial awareness. We cook while planning, listen while solving, rest while worrying. It's not intentional disconnection; it's an inherited habit.

When I slowed down, I started recognizing the pattern beneath the pattern: my family's survival mode disguised as productivity. The doing never stopped because the fear never did. My mother's disconnection wasn't laziness. It was protection. Her absence was how she coped with the weight she carried.

Presence interrupted that cycle. It helped me see that awareness is the first act of freedom. When I became fully conscious in my own body, I could sense when I was slipping into old energy: fixing, controlling, rescuing. Instead of reacting, I could breathe. Instead of forcing, I could feel.

That awareness became a sacred inheritance. What once felt like chaos began to feel like choice. The pattern had always been unconscious living. The new pattern is embodied awareness. Presence revealed that peace was never something to find; it was something to remember.

LUXENARY BRIDGE: Your Next Evolution

Your transition into the next spiral point

Presence is where the old survival patterns finally loosen their grip. It's where you stop rushing, stop fixing, stop performing, and instead meet yourself with truth, compassion, and a full-body exhale. Searching opened your eyes. Presence opened your body. And once you learn to *stay*, to breathe, to witness yourself without judgment, you create space for something deeper to rise.

The next chapter leads you into **Freedom and Union**. The spiral point where presence becomes power. Here, your clarity expands into liberation. The habits, expectations, and inherited patterns that once shaped your identity no longer define you. You begin choosing your life from wholeness rather than wounds.

If presence is returning home to yourself, freedom is learning to live there.

You're awakening and ascending.

REFLECTION PROMPTS (Presence Embodiment)

Use these prompts to deepen your Presence Embodiment work:

1. Where in your life do you move through the motions without truly being present?

2. What inherited patterns of disconnection or avoidance do you now recognize in yourself?

3. When was the last time you felt fully here — in your body, your breath, your now?

4. How does distraction show up in your day-to-day life, and what emotion might it be protecting you from?

5. What simple daily ritual could help you return to presence — breathing, pausing, walking, or stillness?

6. How might your relationships shift if you began listening to understand rather than to respond?

7. What does "embodied awareness" look like for you in moments of tension or uncertainty?

8. If your descendants could feel the peace you cultivate through your presence, what would you want that energy to teach them?

DAWNISM

"Presence is the ultimate luxury."

AFFIRMATIONS

I choose to be fully here in my life. My breath grounds me in safety and truth. Presence is my power, and I return to it with ease. I honor my lineage by living consciously, not automatically.

CHAPTER 13

> "Peace is the woman who stops abandoning herself."

DAWNISM

Dawn M. Rivers

Chapter 13

THE DAY I STOPPED TRYING TO SAVE HER AND STARTED SAVING MYSELF

You don't have to save her

Freedom is knowing you have done your best regardless of what others think about the situation. I had returned to the cycle of people pleasing and concerned about what others thought if I was "a good daughter" or not.

It didn't matter if others had amazing relationships with their mothers, or took care of their mothers for ten years before they passed. This wasn't my job or journey. I love my mother, and I have seen her be strong, resilient, and resourceful. It hurt my heart to see her give up first when my stepfather died and then break again when she gave up on life because she had diminished eyesight because of her stroke. I wanted us to have a better relationship at this stage in our lives. I wanted her to impart grandmotherly wisdom to my children. I wanted her to be around for her great grandchildren when they were born.

Now I know I can only live for myself. I couldn't stop my former husband from drinking or doing drugs. I couldn't tell my children where to live or what their career paths should be. And I couldn't make my mom be different than she was, be happy, or want to live longer.

The Moment I Chose My Freedom

Freedom is knowing you have done your best regardless of what others think about the situation.

For years, I measured my worth through other people's satisfaction, especially my mother's. I carried her expectations like invisible weights, believing that if I could make her proud or comfortable, I would finally earn peace. But peace that depends on someone else's response isn't peace; it's performance.

After her stroke, I found myself slipping back into the old rhythm of fixing, managing, and over-functioning. I wanted to be the "good daughter," the one who made everything right. But there came a moment, a quiet, clear moment, when I realized that my care had become controlling, and my love had turned into labor. I was trying to heal her in the way I wished someone had healed me.

That realization broke something open. It wasn't guilt; it was grace. I saw that I couldn't save my mother from her choices any more than she could have saved me from mine. The work wasn't to change her; it was to change how I carried her story.

Freedom came when I stopped trying to rewrite her ending and started writing my own.

In my mother's generation, love often looked like sacrifice. Boundaries were mistaken for betrayal, silence for strength, and suffering for devotion. But my generation has the opportunity, and responsibility, to love differently. To honor where we came from without repeating the pain that shaped us.

I see it now in the way I live. My home feels lighter. My relationships breathe easier. My decisions no longer orbit around guilt or duty but alignment and peace. The cycle broke not through confrontation, but through compassion.

I no longer need to prove my goodness through exhaustion. I don't measure my success through how well I manage others' emotions. Freedom, for me, is knowing I can love deeply without losing myself.

Integration means I've stopped swinging between extremes, between rebellion and rescue, between independence and obligation. I can honor my mother's humanity and my own. I can live in truth and tenderness at the same time.

That's the real inheritance: not her pain, but her perseverance, transformed into peace.

WHERE ARE YOU NOW?

A moment of honest reflection before you begin

I MIGHT BE STAGNANT STELLA IF...

- ☐ I feel stuck but I'm not sure why
- ☐ I keep saying I'll change when the time is right
- ☐ I feel like life is happening to me
- ☐ I struggle to follow through on decisions
- ☐ I know something is missing but I can't name it

I MIGHT BE SEARCHING SERENA IF...

- ☐ I've read all the books and I'm still in the same place
- ☐ I make progress and then slide back
- ☐ I understand the concepts but can't seem to live them
- ☐ I feel like I'm always one thing away from breakthrough
- ☐ I'm exhausted from trying so hard

I'M STEPPING INTO THRIVING THERESA IF...

- ☐ I am ready to stop performing and start living
- ☐ I want alignment, not just achievement
- ☐ I am willing to look at what I've been carrying
- ☐ I believe my healing can shift my whole family
- ☐ I am ready to feel happy, whole, and free

Wherever you are is exactly where you need to be.

Where are you now?

THE INHERITED BLUEPRINT: The Generational Cycle You Were Born to Break

Every family carries unspoken contracts. Some are built on silence, others on survival. Most are inherited without consent. These contracts shape how we love, how we lead, and how we limit ourselves. They whisper, *"This is how it's always been done."*

My mother's contract was endurance. She believed love meant staying, no matter the cost. My grandmother's was silence: keep your head down, don't make waves, and bear it quietly. I inherited both. For years, I believed that resilience was my superpower. But I eventually learned that resilience without rest becomes resistance to peace.

Each generation in my family mastered survival in its own way, but none of us were taught how to live freely. Freedom wasn't modeled. It had to be imagined.

Breaking this generational pattern required understanding that liberation isn't rebellion; it's reconciliation. It's not about rejecting where you came from but integrating what you've learned so you can evolve the legacy. That's what *Samadhi,* or union, really means. It's the merging of all the parts: the past, the present, the purpose.

When you reach this stage of the spiral, you realize healing was never about erasing your history. It was about transforming your relationship with it. The same patterns that once triggered you now teach you. The same stories that once hurt you now humble you. You no longer need to fight your lineage; you become the bridge that connects its wisdom to its freedom.

Our mothers and grandmothers did what they could with what they knew. Their resilience and repression were both acts of survival. But now, we get to choose a new form of strength. One rooted in awareness rather than endurance.

Generational healing doesn't mean everyone in your family will change. It means *you* change how the story continues. You learn to hold love without losing yourself, to honor the past without being ruled by it, to create peace without waiting for permission.

When you live in union with yourself, your truth, your values, and your divinity, you set the whole lineage free. Your ancestors rest easier because they see that what they started, you are completing. The legacy becomes whole again.

Samadhi Is Enlightenment and Coming Home.

Samadhi is often described as enlightenment, but in lived experience, it feels more like integration. It's the moment when all the work, all the healing, all the awareness finally settles into the body. You're not chasing peace anymore. You've become it.

In yoga philosophy, *Samadhi* is union: the merging of the self with the sacred. It's not an escape from the human experience; it's the embodiment of it. It's when the boundaries between spirit and self dissolve, and life becomes prayer in motion.

For generations, women in our families have known survival but not wholeness. They've known faith, but not freedom. They've carried both strength and sorrow, often at the same time. Our mothers prayed for deliverance; we live as the answer to that prayer. Integration is how we honor both their fight and our freedom.

When I finally stopped trying to fix everything and everyone, I realized peace was already present. It had been waiting for me to surrender. That's what integration really is: the willingness to release the need to control what doesn't belong to you. The nervous system relaxes. The heart softens. The spirit expands. You stop living in reaction and start living in rhythm.

Samadhi doesn't mean life is without challenges. It means you no longer meet those challenges from chaos. You move through them with consciousness. You see patterns reappear, but instead of collapsing, you breathe. You recognize that every lesson was preparing you for this level of calm authority. The kind that can't be shaken because it's rooted in truth.

The earlier phases of the spiral taught awareness, alignment, and action. But integration is different. It's where doing gives way to being. You no longer need to prove your growth; you simply live it.

This stage is where self-leadership becomes legacy. You no longer seek validation from family, community, or culture. You create a new energetic standard. You model emotional maturity, spiritual depth, and grounded joy.

And in this way, you lead, not through striving, but through embodiment.

Integration is also the reunion of your inner parts: the child who needed safety, the woman who needed space, the leader who needed softness. All of them come home. The fragmentation ends. You begin to live as one aligned whole, guided by both wisdom and grace.

In practical terms, this looks like knowing when to speak and when to be silent. It's having clarity without control, purpose without pressure, love without attachment. It's saying: *I trust my path, I release the past, and I live in peace.*

This is the true freedom that transcends generations. It's not found in external success, relationships, or roles; it's the quiet knowing that you are already whole.

When you embody *Samadhi*, you become the calm in your family's story. The chaos stops with you. The striving ends with you. The lineage learns, through you, that rest is safe and peace is possible.

And that is the legacy: not perfection, but presence; not achievement, but alignment. Freedom is not what you earn; it's who you remember yourself to be.

The Spiral Revelation

After years of working with these eight elements, I realized something profound: they don't unfold in a straight line. They spiral. Transformation doesn't happen once; it revisits you, deepens you, refines you. Every insight, every boundary, every breath returns in a new form at a higher level of awareness.

This revelation changed everything.

What I once thought of as a sequence of lessons revealed itself as a living, breathing cycle: a sacred rhythm of remembrance. Each element, from *Refined Integrity* to *Freedom & Union*, builds upon the others, not as a checklist but as an evolution. Together, they create an upward spiral of transformation, one that heals the individual and entire family lines.

The more I studied my clients, my students, and my own life, the more I saw it: awareness leads to affirmation; affirmation leads to aligned action; aligned action leads back to awareness, but from a higher vantage point. It's never about perfection; it's about progression. You rise, you recalibrate, and then you rise again.

That's when *The Luxe Identity Spiral*™ was born.

It began as my personal roadmap for breaking generational patterns, an internal compass for remembering who I was beneath conditioning and chaos. But over time, it evolved into something far greater: a systematic method for generational healing and conscious leadership.

The Spiral is a map for becoming. It guides women from awareness to embodiment, from survival to sovereignty. It honors the truth that growth is not linear, hustle is not holy, and peace is not passive. It's a living framework that allows women to re-enter the same lessons with deeper compassion and more refined consciousness.

Each ascent through the Spiral is both personal and ancestral. Every time you forgive, you lighten your lineage. Every time you rest, you rewrite the rhythm your family once called survival. Every time you choose alignment over approval, you send freedom forward through time.

The Spiral became my life's work because it gave structure to something sacred, proof that spiritual transformation can be both mystical and methodical.

And that's the legacy of this book: not to hand you answers, but to offer you a framework for remembering your own.

The Spiral is not a staircase; it's an ascension. You don't climb it by striving; you rise by surrendering. You spiral upward by integrating your truth again and again, each time closer to freedom, each time more at peace.

What started as my story has become our shared awakening.

And from here, we rise.

LUXE LIFESTYLE RITUAL: The Spiral Integration Practice

Integration is where wisdom becomes lifestyle. It's the quiet rhythm that turns healing into harmony, awareness into artistry, and freedom into flow.

This ritual invites you to live The Luxe Identity Spiral™—not as a concept, but as a daily communion with your highest self.

Step 1: The Morning Alignment (Awareness)

- Begin each day with a single conscious breath.

- Before touching your phone or planning your tasks, place a hand over your heart and ask, *"Who do I choose to be today?"*

- This question shifts you from reaction to creation.

- Awareness always begins the ascent.

Step 2: The Midday Recalibration (Affirmation)

- Pause at midday, between what's behind you and what's ahead, and whisper your truth out loud.

- Say, *"I am aligned. I am guided. I am enough."*

- Affirmation is not about convincing; it's about calibrating.

- Every word you speak becomes an energetic command to the Universe.

Step 3: The Evening Embodiment (Action)

Before bed, reflect on how you lived your values that day. Ask yourself:

- Where did I move in alignment with my truth?

- Where did I resist, and what can I soften tomorrow?

- Then write one conscious act you'll take next—a simple, grounded action that mirrors your awareness.

Step 4: The Weekly Spiral Reflection

- Each week, revisit the eight elements of your journey: Integrity, Rituals, Confidence, Mastery, Stillness, Focus, Presence, and Freedom.

- Notice which one feels most alive and which one is calling for attention.

- The Spiral is alive; it rotates with you.

- Let your energy show you where you are being invited to grow.

Step 5: The Sacred Celebration

- Once a month, celebrate your evolution.

- Light a candle, pour your favorite tea or wine, and write a letter of gratitude to your former self.

- Acknowledge the woman who kept showing up.

- Integration is not a finish line; it's a lifestyle of reverence.

Through this ritual, you live your healing in real time. You spiral upward not by striving, but by returning—to awareness, to truth, to peace.

This is what luxury truly means: living fully, freely, and consciously.

PATTERN RECOGNITION BOX

As I reached this point in my journey, I began to see the pattern within all patterns: every lesson I'd ever learned was leading me back to union. What I thought were cycles of chaos were actually spirals of awakening. Each return to the same theme—boundaries, peace, worth—wasn't repetition; it was refinement.

Integration showed me that nothing had been wasted. The heartbreaks, the detours, the seasons of stillness; they were all working together to bring me home to myself. Freedom wasn't something I found; it was what remained when I stopped running from the truth.

In the beginning, I thought the Spiral was about transformation. Now I know it's about return.

Return to peace.
Return to purpose.
Return to God.

The deeper I practiced, the more I noticed this in my clients, too. Their breakthroughs weren't random. They were rhythmic. They would rise, rest, release, and rise again.

That's when I understood: evolution is never linear. It's sacredly circular.

The Spiral revealed that healing is not about becoming someone new; it's about remembering who you've always been. And when you live from that remembrance, you no longer chase freedom. You embody it.

LUXENARY BRIDGE: Your Next Evolution

Freedom is the moment your healing stops being something you work on and becomes the way you live. Samadhi isn't perfection; it's integration. The merging of all the versions of you that survived, stretched, searched, and surrendered to growth. And when you reach this point, life begins to respond to your wholeness differently.

This is where the spiral widens into legacy. Where your transformation stops being personal and becomes generational. This is where the spiral widens into legacy, where your transformation stops being personal and becomes generational, where the woman you've become starts shaping the future of every woman who comes after you..

In the next (and final) section, you'll step into the epilogue, the place where you name the legacy you're building, honor the ancestors who carried you this far, and articulate the future you are consciously creating. If Samadhi is union, the epilogue is expression: the beginning of the life that only you can write.

You are ready.

You are whole.

You are free, and now, you become the one who leads others into their freedom.

REFLECTION PROMPTS (Freedom & Union — Samadhi)

Use these prompts to integrate your transformation and anchor your legacy:

1. How do you now define freedom, not as escape, but as embodiment?

2. What patterns have officially ended with you? How can you tell?

3. What have you forgiven, in yourself, your parents, or your lineage, that once felt impossible?

4. Where do you now choose peace over performance in your daily life?

5. How has your healing created shifts in your family system, even if others haven't changed?

6. What does it feel like to lead with calm authority instead of fear, guilt, or obligation?

7. How do you honor the child you were while still evolving the woman you're becoming?

8. What legacy of wholeness, rest, and alignment do you want your descendants to inherit?

DAWNISM

"Peace is the woman who stops abandoning herself."

AFFIRMATIONS

I choose peace as my home and my heritage. I am no longer shaped by the patterns I inherited. I breathe in freedom and breathe out legacy.I honor my ancestors by living fully, freely, and consciously. I am whole. I am aligned. I am complete.

PART THREE

LIVING LIMITLESSLY

*This is what changes
when you do.*

Chapter 14

WHEN ONE WOMAN HEALS, A WHOLE FAMILY SHIFTS

It didn't stop with you.

There are moments in this work when you witness a woman cross an invisible threshold. She steps out of who she has been, and into who she was always meant to be. Her voice softens. Her shoulders drop. Her eyes widen with the realization that she can choose a different life than the one she inherited. And when that shift happens for one woman, it rarely ends with her. It ripples. It moves. It reaches her children, her partners, her friendships, her lineage. This is the quiet, steady miracle of generational transformation.

I think back to the very first woman who ever asked me to mentor her. Melissa had finished her yoga teacher training, attended my first retreat, and joined my studio team. She pulled me aside one day and said, "I want to launch my yoga business. Can you help me?" We met every week, building her offer, carving out her brand, clarifying her voice. Melissa was a single mother who wanted her daughter to witness a woman creating a life from purpose, passion, and persistence. She had done graphic design on the side for years, but yoga ignited something deeper. A calling. A remembering.

What struck me then is what I still see today: a woman doesn't come to me because everything is falling apart; she comes because something inside her refuses to remain the same. Many of these women had reached crossroads. They were either ready to start businesses, heal long-standing wounds with their children, reclaim their identities after major transitions, or dissolve patterns they had carried since girlhood. They were ready to begin again.

These stories are about transformation. They are about trajectory. These women didn't simply change their lives. **They changed the lives of everyone who comes after them.**

Celeste's Turning Point

Before Celeste ever reached out to me, she had already lived a full lifetime of navigating struggle. Raised in a family where survival was valued more than self-expression, she learned early to keep moving, keep working, keep pushing. Her relationships reflected the same patterns: difficult, unstable, rooted in old wounds she had inherited rather than created. She was brilliant, intuitive, and gifted, but stuck in a familiar loop of chaos and self-doubt.

By the time she found her way into my coaching container, Celeste had recently relocated thousands of miles away from the place she grew up. It was a bold choice, one driven by both necessity and desire. She wanted a different life for her teenage son, and she wanted a different life for herself. But distance doesn't dissolve patterns. She carried many of them with her.

In our work together, we didn't have the Spiral yet. What we had was the Path to the Awakened Woman Framework. The foundation of everything I now teach. We focused on awareness, identity, truth, and the courage to choose differently. Session by session, Celeste learned to interrupt her automatic reactions. She started recognizing when she was choosing partners from fear rather than worthiness. She began to understand how deeply her upbringing shaped her self-concept. She learned to pause, breathe, and ask herself the questions she had never been taught to consider:

"Do I feel safe here?"

"Is this love or familiarity?"

"Am I shrinking to keep the peace?"

"What would I choose if I trusted my future self?"

One of the most profound moments in her journey happened long after our formal coaching ended. I visited her city during a vacation, and we met for dinner. She arrived with her former partner, a person she had rekindled a relationship with. Throughout the evening, I watched her closely. I saw her partner's possessive energy, subtle comments, small withdrawals of approval. I also saw Celeste's eyes: quiet, observant, discerning. She wasn't shrinking. She wasn't bending. She wasn't performing.

She was studying the dynamic.

And within weeks, she ended it.

That choice, to walk away not because she was broken, but because she was finally whole, is what marked the beginning of her new identity. Celeste stood on her own two feet, not in defiance, but in truth. She made decisions from clarity rather than fear. She stopped choosing partners who mirrored her past and began choosing experiences that matched her future.

Over the next year, she built a life she once thought was impossible. She moved to the exact city she had dreamed of while we were coaching together. She built stability. She rebuilt confidence. She learned how to self-soothe, self-trust, and self-direct. And perhaps most beautifully, her son followed her into the very field she entered when she first moved away. He grew up watching a mother transform her entire life, and he stepped into adulthood with a sense of purpose, resilience, and possibility she never had at his age.

The legacy of Celeste's transformation is her new beginning.

It is the generational path she carved for her son.

A path without the struggle she had to endure.

A path with modeling rather than martyrdom.

A path shaped by choice rather than circumstance.

When I look back, the Spiral was already at work in her, long before I named it or designed it. She practiced *Awareness* by seeing her patterns. She practiced *Alignment* by ending a relationship that no longer matched who she was becoming. She practiced *Ascension* by building a life rooted in self-trust.

Celeste was an Awakened Woman before she ever knew the language. Her story is proof that when one woman chooses herself, **an entire lineage rises with her.**

Priya's Journey back to herself

Before Priya ever stepped into my coaching space, she had already lived through several lifetimes of reinvention. Raised in a small suburban community as a Muslim girl with strict expectations, she spent her early years learning how to shrink, comply, and stay within the rules of her faith and family culture. But she also carried a fire inside her; one that refused to go out, no matter how often life tried to dim it.

By her teens, that fire turned into rebellion. She became a mother earlier than she expected and had to grow up fast. The weight of responsibility, judgment, and limited resources shaped her early adulthood. Later, she married and had two more children. But the relationships with her children's fathers repeated the same painful cycles: emotional abandonment, inconsistency, moments of abuse that left their marks, and seasons of survival that hardened her spirit.

Yet Priya had a gift, one passed down from her father and the long line of knitters in her family. She learned how to make simple knitted and crocheted hats as a young girl. She learned how to design patterns instinctively, how to create afghans and throws with unique colors combinations. As she grew older, she realized knitting was more than a hobby for her. It was identity. It was expression. It was freedom.

So she became an artisan.

A trained, talented, handicrafts person who took risks and dreamed loudly. She designed, experimented with different types of materials, invented her own design combinations, and built a business that became locally known and deeply loved. She worked long hours, a full-time job during the day, her business on evenings and weekends, and motherhood woven between every minute.

For a while, she held it all together.

Until she couldn't.

Like so many entrepreneurs, her business hit a slow season. The revenue dropped. The clients dwindled. The exhaustion caught up. And the weight of raising her children alone, physically, emotionally, and financially, became too much. She lost her apartment and moved back in with her father. Her youngest children's father and his wife asked if they could take the children during that season. Out of honesty and exhaustion, Priya agreed.

She told me later that this was the lowest point of her life.

Not because she failed, but because she felt like she'd become the woman she swore she would never be.

She was drowning in shame, guilt, and the fear that her children would see her differently.

That is when she came back to me.

We had worked together off and on for years, but this time was different. She wasn't looking for brand strategy or business coaching. She was searching for identity, grounding, clarity. She wanted to rebuild, but in a way that didn't cost her her peace. When we sat together earlier that year, she didn't need a marketing plan. She needed a lifeline.

We created one.

We mapped out a plan for her weekends with her children: low-cost adventures that didn't require her to pretend she had more than she did. She found joy in the simplicity of creating memories instead of artifacts. We talked honestly about her finances, her fears, and her worth. We explored the cycles she had inherited: money scarcity, hyper-independence, overworking, and the constant belief that she had to sacrifice herself to prove she was a good mother.

And piece by piece, she began to stand again.

She found work as an artisan.
She rebuilt her stability.
She showed up for her healing.
She reconnected with her creativity.
She forgave herself.
She learned to trust again.

Recently, a mutual friend told me Priya had moved into her own apartment. After years of chaos, loss, rebuilding, and resilience, she rose again. Not in the loud, flashy way she once thought success required but in the quiet, steady way that creates generational impact.

Her children, now older, see a mother who didn't give up. Who kept choosing them even when she could not choose convenience. Who kept believing in herself even when life broke her open.

Priya is someone who falls down and gets back up every time. And now, on more solid ground than ever, she is beginning a new chapter. One marked not only by strength, but by **wisdom, maturity, and possibility**.

This time, she isn't building from survival. She is building from self-worth. And that shift, that internal rewiring, is the real generational wealth she is creating for her children.

Sloane Sees Herself

Some women arrive in your coaching space with a glow that only needs direction. Sloane was one of those women. A writer, a marketer, a creative with depth and spirit, she had a mind full of ideas, a heart full of compassion, and a life full of obligations. From the outside, she looked accomplished: respected at work, deeply connected to her family, admired among her peers. But underneath the surface, she was carrying an internal storm of overwhelm, fear-based decision-making, and fragmented focus.

When we first met for a 90-minute session, she talked fast. She had a dozen projects, three new business ideas, two books she wanted to write, and a growing list of obligations she couldn't keep up with. She was already doing so much, yet still felt behind. This is the classic signature of a Searching Serena, a woman whose brilliance becomes scattered because she's unsure which version of herself to commit to.

Over time, our work together deepened. She enrolled in private coaching, then later joined my six-month Awakened Woman Academy. But even with dedicated containers, Sloane struggled to narrow her focus. Every idea that came to her felt urgent, meaningful, and possible. She didn't want to disappoint her family, her clients, or herself. She didn't want to pick "wrong." And beneath all that mental activity was a quiet truth she rarely spoke aloud:

She didn't fully trust that one offering, one path, one message from her would be enough.

Searching Serenas often default to busyness as a shield, a way to avoid the vulnerability of choosing one thing and letting themselves be seen in it. Sloane mastered that shield. During our sessions we would map out a clear step, and within a week she would be pulled into a family obligation, a work crisis, or a new idea that felt more exciting than the one she committed to.

But what made her story compelling wasn't the struggle. It was the glimpses of profound potential underneath.

Sloane's talent was undeniable. Her writing had emotional depth. Her marketing instinct was sharp. Her ideas were meaningful. And more than anything, she carried a gift for helping others tell their stories with dignity and power. The legacy she wanted to build, a legacy rooted in storytelling, generational healing, and creative empowerment, was aligned with the work she was born to do.

Yet every time she approached this truth, fear would rise.

Questions like:

- "Who am I to do this?"

- "What if I fail?"

- "What if it doesn't work?"

- "What if someone else is already doing it better?"

So instead of stepping into her signature offer, she continued juggling everything at once: work projects, business ideas, family responsibilities, and planning for a large social gathering.

In one coaching cycle, she finally named the thing she wanted. The signature offer that lit her up. She outlined it. She described it beautifully. She even smiled with a sense of recognition, as if she had finally remembered a forgotten part of herself.

But naming a desire and embodying it are two different things.

She didn't follow through, not because she lacked ability, but because she needed more time to become the woman who could steward that vision. Transformation isn't linear. Sometimes the most powerful work happens in the seasons where nothing seems to be happening at all.

And even though she wasn't ready to leap, the coaching itself changed her. She began setting boundaries with family. She became more discerning with her time. She stopped saying yes out of guilt. She started honoring her creative energy. She began to see her own gifts with clearer eyes.

These internal shifts will shape her future more than any single launch ever could.

Her children, watching quietly from the sidelines, are learning something important: that a woman can pursue her dreams at any age, that creativity is sacred, that self-worth is not tied to constant productivity, and that clarity often comes through stillness, not speed.

Sloane isn't done. She's still becoming. And when she finally chooses her path and commits to one offering, one message, one doorway into her brilliance...

She will serve thousands. She will change lives. She will become the storyteller and legacy-builder she has always felt called to be.

Not on anyone else's timeline. But on her own.

Zahra's Steps into What's Possible

Some transformations happen in big, dramatic moments. Others unfold quietly, almost imperceptibly, like a slow sunrise. Zahra's journey was the latter: a delicate, tender unraveling of patterns that had shaped the women in her family for generations.

When Zahra first came to me, she was on the edge of retirement, yet she wasn't feeling the freedom most people expect at that stage of life. Instead, she felt stuck between roles she had outgrown and relationships that felt strained, especially with her daughters. There was love, of course, deep, fierce love, but it was tangled with old misunderstandings, unspoken hurts, and a lifetime of unmet expectations.

Mother–daughter dynamics can be some of the most complex, especially when both are carrying wounds handed down by their own mothers. With Zahra, this was unmistakably present. Her desire for connection often collided with her daughters' desire for independence. Their conversations felt loaded. Their silences felt louder. Their bond needed healing, but neither knew how to initiate it.

During our work together, I coached Zahra and her oldest daughter separately, but during the same chapter of their lives. This made the work emotionally layered. Each woman was seeking something slightly different. Each carried different stories about the past. Each longed for closeness but wasn't sure how to get there. Coaching them side by side revealed something powerful: generational patterns rarely begin with the people who are struggling to navigate them. They begin long before.

One of the most striking themes in Zahra's sessions was how much she carried: the weight of her marriage, the emotional demands of motherhood, the pressure to be strong even when she was tired, and the fear of admitting that she wanted something more. She had spent decades caring for everyone else, and by the time she reached retirement age, she barely knew how to care for herself without guilt.

But even in her exhaustion, she showed up. She listened. She reflected. She cried. She took responsibility for her growth. She began to see her own patterns clearly: the tendency to hold onto hurt, the fear of expressing her needs, the habit of putting herself last. These small moments of recognition were some of the most significant breakthroughs of her journey.

Still, transformation is not always a clean, immediate shift. When our coaching time ended, I could tell Zahra was still in the early stages of her healing. She was afraid: afraid of rocking the boat, afraid of initiating hard conversations, afraid of losing the relationships she cherished most. She was sad, grieving the years she could not get back. And she was tired. The bone-deep fatigue of a woman who has carried more than her share for far too long.

But she was not without tools. She had awareness now. The first step in any generational shift.

She had language for her emotions.
She had new boundaries she was learning to vocalize.
She had compassion for herself and her daughters.
She had the ability to pause instead of react.

These subtle shifts matter. Sometimes the biggest transformation is simply recognizing the pattern, because once a woman sees it, she can never unsee it again. And that alone begins to soften the pattern's power.

Even though Zahra and I have not spoken recently, I believe she is still in her spiral. Still learning. Still practicing. Still becoming. And even if she feels stuck at times, she is not where she used to be.

She is now the cycle-breaker of her family, not because she has completed her healing, but because she has chosen to face it.

And that choice, even imperfectly lived, changes everything for the women who come after her.

Natalia Learns Her Gifts Have Value

Every coach has those clients whose stories stay with them for years. Women whose transformation is not loud or flashy, but deeply rooted and profoundly generational. Natalia's journey is one of those stories. Her healing unfolded slowly, steadily, and with a kind of quiet courage that deserved to be witnessed.

When Natalia first crossed my path, she was juggling more than most people could imagine. She was a full-time C-suite executive, a mother of four children, including one with special needs, and a woman who had been carrying the emotional weight of her family for decades. She wanted to enroll in my Yoga Teacher Training, but her schedule simply would not allow it. Between work, caregiving, and the demands of daily life, she could not add one more thing to her overflowing plate.

Still, she found a way to follow the pull.

She eventually discovered a teacher training program that fit her schedule and completed it with the same determination she brought to every part of her life. For Natalia, yoga was not simply a hobby. It was an anchor. A way of coming home to herself after years of giving everything to everyone else.

After training, she became a teacher in the community: skilled, thoughtful, and deeply committed to holding space for others. But yoga wasn't the end of her evolution. It was the beginning.

Over time, she began exploring other healing modalities. She studied Reiki. She learned the art of energy work. And then she discovered sound healing, a practice that awakened something ancient in her. Natalia fell in love with the crystal bowls, the chimes, the rain sticks, the resonant tones that could shift the nervous system with a single strike. She learned how to create sound journeys that felt like medicine. She practiced. She invested. She studied more.

She kept going.

But behind all of this growth was something else happening quietly: her marriage was crumbling. For years she had been the giver, the one who accommodated, soothed, supported, and held everything together. She had lost herself in the process. She was exhausted, unseen, emotionally starved. The woman who held space for everyone else had no one holding space for her.

Her healing work brought clarity she could no longer ignore.
Sound healing awakened her voice.
Reiki awakened her intuition.
Yoga awakened her body's truth.

By her early forties, she realized she could no longer remain in a marriage where her needs were dismissed and her spirit was dimmed. She began preparing to leave, not out of anger, but out of self-preservation.

That's when she came to me again, this time not as a yoga teacher but as a woman in transition. We worked on her money wounds, deeply rooted beliefs shaped by culture, family, religion, and decades of putting others first. Despite her years as an executive, she struggled to charge appropriately for her healing work. She could justify expenses on behalf of the company she worked for, which felt rational and socially acceptable, but found herself shrinking when it came to charging for her gifts.

"It feels indulgent," she once told me.

"It feels like I'm asking for too much."

This is a common pattern among women who are natural healers: they undervalue what cannot be quantified by degrees or titles. They forget that wisdom earned through lived experience is still wisdom. They forget that the years spent studying energy work, trauma responses, and somatic healing are as legitimate as any traditional education.

Natalia had spent thousands of dollars on her training. She invested in bowls, chimes, mats, blankets, bolsters, everything she needed to create the sound experiences she dreamed of. She carried these items from studio to studio, office to office, retreat to retreat. She said yes to every gig, every workshop, every opportunity to share her gift.

But she struggled to believe she was worthy of being compensated for it.

Our work together was about reframing that story, helping her understand that her healing work was not an "extra," but an essential. Her sessions transformed people. Her presence shifted energy. Her voice soothed trauma. Her gift mattered.

And slowly, she began to believe that.

She upgraded her pricing. She upgraded her environment. She upgraded her standards.

She outgrew the small room in the small space she rented and began to envision herself as *the* sound healer of her region: a leader, a guide, a woman who held sacred space with authority and grace.

Her personal life shifted alongside her professional one. As she separated from her husband and began rebuilding her life, her daughters watched her with wide eyes. They saw a mother who chose her joy after decades of self-sacrifice. A mother who created beauty from resilience. A mother who dared to break generational patterns of silence, submission, and self-denial.

Her daughters learned this truth through her example:

- A woman is allowed to choose herself.

- A woman is allowed to be happy.

- A woman is allowed to create a life that reflects her truth.

Natalia's evolution wasn't loud. It wasn't linear. It wasn't fast. But it was sacred.

She is still building. Still rising. Still discovering herself. But one thing is certain: she has awakened.

And because of her, her daughters will never have to question what an awakened woman looks like.

THE PATTERN OF TRANSFORMATION

When you look at these stories side by side, a clear pattern emerges: a pattern that appears every time a woman chooses to interrupt the cycles she inherited. What Celeste, Priya, Sloane, Zahra, Melissa, and Natalia all have in common is not their backgrounds, their personalities, or their circumstances. It is the moment each of them finally said, "I cannot live like this anymore." That moment is the doorway. That moment is the portal. That moment is the beginning of generational change.

Cycle-breaking is not random. It is not accidental. It follows a predictable path that I have now seen in women across cultures, ages, professions, and life stages. First comes **awareness** — the ability to see the pattern clearly and tell the truth about it. Then comes **identity work** — the shifting, questioning, and unlearning that makes new choices possible. After that comes **alignment** — the stage where behavior begins to match intention, boundaries solidify, and relationships recalibrate. And finally comes **ascension**, the internal freedom that allows a woman to live from truth instead of trauma.

This is the pattern.
This is the Spiral.
This is the work.

What makes this chapter powerful is not that these women transformed; it's that their transformations rippled outward. Celeste's son followed a new path because she forged one. Priya's children witnessed resilience instead of resignation. Sloane's family are growing up watching a woman honor her creativity instead of her fear. Zahra's daughters will heal in ways she could not. Melissa's daughter saw her mother build something from nothing. Natalia's daughters learned that a woman's joy is not optional.

Their healing became their legacy.

And witnessing these patterns again and again is what showed me something essential:

What started as individual coaching had become a replicable system for generational transformation. A system other women, coaches, healers, guides, and leaders, could learn and bring into their own communities.

These case studies aren't merely stories.

They're blueprints.
They're breadcrumbs.
They're the foundation for the work that comes next.

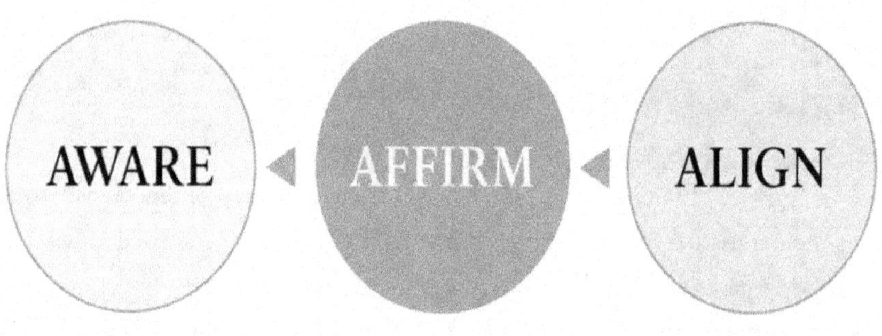

THE LUXE IDENTITY SPIRAL™

AWARE • AFFIRM • ALIGN

AWARE	AFFIRM	ALIGN
See the patterns you've been living in	Reclaim the truth of who you are	Build the life that finally feels like yours

ROOTED IN THE EIGHT LIMBS OF YOGA

AWARE	AFFIRM	ALIGN
Yamas • Niyamas • Asana	Pranayama • Pratyahara • Dharana	Dhyana • Samadhi

You are not broken. You are becoming.

The Luxe Identity Spiral

LUXENARY Breadcrumbs

These women changed their lives. They showed me, again and again, that transformation follows a pattern, a rhythm, a sequence of awakening that can be taught, repeated, and scaled. Their stories revealed something I didn't fully understand in the early years of my coaching:

These transformations showed me that a complete certification system was needed.

What began as intimate one-on-one work, private sessions, and personal breakthroughs slowly revealed a deeper truth. I was not simply coaching individual women; I was uncovering a structure, a pathway, a methodology that reliably moved people from survival to sovereignty.

What started as individual coaching became a replicable method for generational healing.

I began to see the same milestones, the same emotional shifts, the same identity pivots show up across women of different ages, cultures, and life experiences. Whether they were rebuilding relationships, breaking money patterns, reclaiming their voices, or creating businesses from purpose rather than fear. The transformation moved through a recognizable spiral.

- Awareness.

- Identity.

- Alignment.

- Ascension.

Over and over, the same upward movement.

And as my work expanded, so did my vision. It became clear that the world didn't need more coaching and it needed **more coaches who knew how to facilitate generational change without burning out, bypassing emotions, or relying on guesswork.**

I realized other coaches and healers needed these tools to create systematic transformation in their communities.

The Luxe Identity Spiral™ was more than my framework. It was becoming a lighthouse, a structure designed to train leaders, guides, and cycle-breakers who could bring this work into homes, studios, classrooms, congregations, and healing spaces.

These stories mark the end of one chapter, and the beginning of a new evolution of leadership.

THE POWER OF RENAMING: Honoring Their Journeys

Names carry energy. They hold meaning, history, symbolism, and identity. As I prepared these stories for this book, I chose to rename each woman, not to erase who they are, but to **protect their privacy and honor the essence of their transformation**. Each new name was chosen intentionally, aligned with the deeper truth of their journeys and the legacy they are now creating.

These aren't random placeholders; they're archetypal. They're symbolic. They're rooted in the spirit of who these women became.

Celeste

Celeste means "heavenly" and "of the sky." It reflects her rise, her ability to lift herself out of generational struggle and create a new life built on self-worth. She represents elevation, clarity, and the kind of transformation that ripples upward through a family line.

Priya

Priya means "beloved." Her story is one of rebuilding self-love after seasons of hardship, shame, survival, and reinvention. She reclaimed her identity, her stability, and her hope. Her new name reminds us that resilience is rooted in love and becomes a legacy for her children.

Sloane

Sloane carries the energy of strength and tenacity. It symbolizes the inner warrior in her. The woman fighting through overwhelm, fear, and scattered dreams to discover her true calling. She represents the women who are still becoming, still unfolding, still remembering.

Zahra

Zahra means "flower," "blossom," and "shining." Her journey is quiet, tender, and brave. She is the woman in the slow bloom healing at her own pace, breaking patterns quietly, and becoming the cycle-breaker her lineage needed.

Melissa

Melissa means "honeybee," a symbol of devotion, purpose, and building something sweet and lasting. Her story reflects the early seasons of your leadership. The women who trusted you before you had a framework, a brand, or a methodology.

Natalia

Natalia means "birth" and "awakening," perfect for a woman who rebuilt her life from the inside out. She chose her happiness. She chose her truth. She chose to break generational patterns of silence. Her name honors her rebirth.

Dara

Dara means "wisdom" and "compassion." Her journey represents the inner awakening of Thriving Theresa. The moment a woman realizes she is no longer who she used to be, and she steps fully into her sovereignty.

Renaming these women was more than a protective measure. It was an act of alignment, a way of honoring the archetypal essence of each journey and preserving the sacredness of their stories.

Their real names belong to their lived experiences. These new names belong to the **legacy** of their transformation.

Each woman becomes both herself and an emblem, a symbol of the countless women who see themselves reflected in these stories. They represent the Celestes, Priyas, Sloanes, Zahras, Melissas, Natalias, and Daras who are rising every day, quietly shifting their lives and their lineage.

And in the renaming, we acknowledge something profound:

Transformation changes a woman's circumstances. It changes the way she's known: by herself, by her family, and by the world.

This chapter is their tribute. Their honoring. Their imprint on the Spiral.

Chapter 15
NOW THAT WE KNOW BETTER

It didn't end with you. It begins with you.

There is a moment in every cycle-breaker's life when she realizes she is no longer living the story she inherited. For me, that moment didn't arrive as a single revelation. It came in waves: a slow, steady awakening that stretched across years, motherhood, loss, truth-telling, and the deep internal work I had avoided for far too long. My transformation did not happen all at once. It spiraled, much like the work I now teach.

I was raised by a mother who loved me, but who carried wounds she never had permission, language, or support to heal. She modeled strength, resilience, and survival. She modeled doing what needed to be done. But she also modeled silence. Self-forgetting. The weight of pleasing. The ache of unspoken dreams. For years, I mistook those patterns for personality. I thought this was simply what womanhood required.

If you become a mother, the child looks at you as their definition of love, truth, and possibility, you begin to see your lineage differently. You begin to ask yourself questions that aren't easy to answer.

Where did this belief come from?

Who taught me to minimize myself?

Why do I feel responsible for everyone's comfort but my own?

Who would I be if I stopped carrying what never belonged to me?

My children were the first mirror I ever truly looked into. They saw strength in me long before I did. They saw brilliance long before I claimed it. They saw a woman who could create magic, even when she doubted herself. And it was through their eyes that I realized I didn't want to pass down the same emotional inheritance I had received.

I wanted more for them. Which meant I had to become more for myself.

Breaking my cycle was about healing from the past and consciously designing the future It was about moving from reaction to intention. From survival to sovereignty. From repeating patterns to rewriting them.

As I stepped deeper into my own healing, I started noticing the changes in my children. They became more expressive, more confident, more willing to try, to dream, to fail without shame. They watched me evolve, not perfectly, but honestly. And that honesty became part of our generational DNA.

Every time I chose truth over guilt, they felt it.

Every time I chose rest over overworking, they saw it.

Every time I honored my intuition, they learned to trust their own.

This is the real legacy of a cycle-breaker: not perfection, but possibility.

My transformation continues even now. I am still learning, unlearning, recalibrating. I am still softening in places where my heart hardened. I am still releasing what never belonged to me. I am still rising into the woman I hope my great-granddaughters speak of with gratitude.

The Spiral is not something I teach because it's clever or structured. I teach it because I lived it. I survived it. I created it because I needed a map myself. And once I found one, I knew it wasn't meant for me alone.

This chapter is about where I've been. It's about where you, and all of us, are going next.

THE VISION FOR GLOBAL IMPACT

There is a point in every leader's journey where the work is no longer limited to her personal journey. As I watched woman after woman rise through her own spiral of healing, a truth became impossible to ignore: **this work is not meant to stay inside one coaching container, one city, or one lifetime.** The change we create individually is powerful, but the change we create collectively is unstoppable.

My vision for global generational healing began quietly. It began the moment

I saw what happened to the children of my clients. How a single shift from one mother would ripple into her home, her lineage, and even her community. How a woman who healed her relationship with money changed the financial DNA of her household. How a woman who learned boundaries raised children who would never settle for less than respect. How a woman who reclaimed her voice birthed a generation who spoke with more strength, clarity, and self-trust.

It was my clients who were transforming. But also their families were transforming. Their communities were transforming. Their futures were transforming.

That's when I realized that one-on-one coaching, while deeply meaningful, would never be enough to meet the scale of what this world needs. Because the truth is this:

One woman rising changes a family.

A circle of women rising changes a community.

A global network of women rising changes the future of humanity.

This is where *Luxenaries* were born as a global movement. A collective of women who live, breathe, and embody generational transformation. Women who choose luxury as alignment rather than excess. Women who lead with compassion and clarity. Women who are rewriting what it means to rise.

Luxenaries are not defined by titles or roles. They are defined by impact. And impact requires a method: something teachable, repeatable, sustainable.

That method became the **Luxe Identity Spiral™**.

I didn't build the Spiral so I could have a signature framework. I built it because I needed a way to explain what I had been witnessing for years: a predictable, transformational sequence that emerged across cultures, ages, backgrounds, and stories. A spiral that reflected the multidimensional nature of healing. A path that honored the truth that every woman rises in cycles, not straight lines.

But as the Spiral grew, so did the demand.

Women weren't only asking for coaching anymore.

- They were asking to learn the method.

- They were asking to facilitate the work.

- They were asking how to bring these tools into their own families, communities, churches, schools, and healing spaces.

- They weren't asking for inspiration.

- They were asking for **training**.

That is when I understood something critical:
If we want sustainable generational change, we must train the women who are called to lead it.

Coaches, healers, therapists, wellness practitioners, educators, ministry leaders, social workers, community elders — all of them need structures and methods that work. The transformation of one woman is powerful, but the training of thousands of women is how movements are born.

This is why certification matters.

Not for prestige.

Not for branding.

Not for trend.

Certification matters because generational healing requires skill, emotional intelligence, and the ability to guide someone through the Spiral without causing harm, spiritual bypassing, or energetic overwhelm. It requires depth. It requires tools. It requires a leader who has walked the path herself.

The world does not need more untrained coaches. The world needs **equipped** ones. Women who facilitate transformation with integrity, compassion, and competence.

My vision is a global network of certified *Luxenaries*. Women who become pillars in their communities, leaders of their families, and guardians of generational healing. Women trained to guide others through the Spiral with precision and care.

A global renaissance of healed women, healing women.

A lineage of cycle-breakers who doing more than surviving. They ascend.

And this is where your own path begins to widen.

Because the Spiral didn't stop with me. It won't stop with you. It is meant to continue, globally.

THE COMPLETE SYSTEM REVEALED

For years, I felt the truth of the work long before I could articulate it. I watched women unravel patterns that had shaped their families for generations. I watched their identities shift. I watched their relationships recalibrate. I watched their lives transform so completely that even their children walked differently in the world.

But I didn't have a name for what I was witnessing. Not yet.

I knew it wasn't linear. Healing never is. I knew it wasn't random. The shifts were too consistent. I knew it was emotional and it touched every layer of a woman's life. I knew it wasn't temporary. It rewired their futures.

What I now call the **Luxe Identity Spiral™** began as a question:

Why do some women create lasting change while others repeat the same cycles year after year?

The answer revealed itself slowly through thousands of coaching conversations, yoga teacher trainings, retreats, workshops, and intimate stories of heartbreak, doubt, courage, and awakening.

It wasn't willpower.
It wasn't discipline.
It wasn't motivation.

It was identity.
It was embodiment.
It was energetic alignment.
It was a shift in the way a woman *sees herself.*

I began mapping the patterns.
The emotional signatures.
The behavioral shifts.

The internal milestones that appeared in the same sequence across different women.

> Awareness always came first — the willingness to see the truth.
> Then identity — confronting the stories and roles that no longer fit.
> Then alignment — rewiring choices, patterns, and boundaries.
> Then ascension — stepping into a higher expression of self.

> A spiral.
> Not a ladder.
> Not a straight path.
> A movement inward and upward.
> A return to self that deepens with each cycle.

The Luxe Identity Spiral™ emerged as a living, breathing system. It was the culmination of my personal healing, my spiritual studies, my years of coaching, and the ancient wisdom embedded in the Eight Limbs of Yoga, the Yamas and Niyamas, chakra philosophy, and modern personal development. It blended all of it into a method that honors the whole woman: mental, emotional, physical, spiritual, and generational.

As I continued refining it, something extraordinary happened: I realized the spiral did not only describe *individual* healing. It described **generational** healing.

Each turn of a woman's spiral influences the spirals of her children, her relationships, and the lineage that follows her.

> A woman who learns boundaries raises children who honor their own.
> A woman who heals her money wounds raises a family that trusts abundance.
> A woman who stops people-pleasing raises daughters who speak their truth.
> A woman who trusts her intuition raises a generation that isn't afraid to follow their inner wisdom.

This is why the Spiral is so powerful. It changes more than one life at a time.

But understanding the Spiral was only the first step. I knew I couldn't keep this work to myself. Not if I wanted the impact to outlive me.

The more I worked with clients, the more I recognized a truth I could not ignore:

This work requires depth.

This work requires training.

This work requires facilitators who can hold space with skill, safety, and intention.

Too many coaching spaces are built on borrowed tools, surface-level strategies, or imitated language without embodied understanding. Generational healing cannot be faked. It cannot be rushed. It cannot be guessed. It must be guided through a proven system by someone who has walked the path herself.

The Luxe Identity Spiral™ became that system: a map, a method, and a movement.

A full framework that includes:

- identity mapping

- emotional pattern decoding

- generational cycle awareness

- energetic and somatic alignment

- lifestyle rituals

- boundary and relationship rewiring

- decision-making architecture

- spiritual integration

- and the upward movement from Awareness to Ascension

But the system doesn't stop with information. It requires **embodiment**. It requires **intuition**. It requires **leadership**.

This is why certification became essential, not optional.

A trained facilitator can walk someone through complex emotions without projecting their own. A certified guide can identify generational patterns without retraumatizing a client. A Luxenary leader knows how to honor cultural nuance, spiritual depth, and emotional safety.

This is the difference between inspiration and transformation.

The Spiral is my work. It is my offering to the world. It is the system I hope will outlive me, taught by women whose names I may never know. It is the women who will carry this flame into communities I may never touch.

Because the future I see is not built by one woman. It is built by thousands.

It is built by Luxenaries.

And the Spiral is how we get there.

THE BRIDGE TO THE NEXT LEVEL

By the time you arrive at this point in the book, something inside you has already shifted. You've recognized patterns you inherited, and you've begun to see how they've shaped your life. You've gathered tools, insights, and language that you may not have had before. You've taken your first steps into conscious awareness, the beginning of your own spiral.

But awareness is only the first gateway.

This book was designed to give you the **foundation** — the clarity, the compassion, and the courage to look at yourself honestly. It offered the early tools, the mindset shifts, the stories, and the practices that begin the healing process. But it was never meant to be the entire system. This book has walked you to the edge of the path, but the deeper journey begins when you step beyond these pages.

Because personal healing is only one half of the Spiral. The other half is leadership.

Many women read books like this for themselves. They want to break cycles, find peace, reclaim identity, heal family patterns, and navigate life with more grace and intention. And that is beautiful. For some women, that is the whole purpose of encountering this work.

But for others, maybe for you, something more begins to stir. As you heal, you start to feel the pull to help others heal, too. As you rise, you begin to imagine what it would look like to lead. As you rewrite your story, you begin to sense that you're meant to guide others through their own spiral of becoming.

This is the natural progression of transformation:

- You move from **student** to **steward**.

- From **seeker** to **guide**.

- From **cycle-breaker** to **cycle-healer**.

And that evolution requires more than inspiration. It requires structure. It requires training. It requires a systematic approach to helping others achieve the kind of breakthroughs you've experienced within these chapters.

The Luxe Identity Spiral™ Certification is not simply "next-level learning." It is the bridge between personal healing and generational impact. It equips you with the tools, the language, the frameworks, the emotional intelligence, and the embodiment practices needed to safely and powerfully guide others.

The work you've done here has opened your eyes.

The deeper work will open your path.

Whether you choose to continue for your own evolution or for the women you're called to serve, this moment, right here, is your crossroads.

You have learned how to rise.

Now, if you choose, you can learn how to lead.

YOUR INVITATION FORWARD

If you feel a stirring inside you right now, trust it. Transformation always brings you to a moment of decision. The moment when who you've become begins calling you into who you are meant to be next. This chapter is not a goodbye. It is an invitation. The Spiral doesn't end here; it widens. And now, you get to choose the path that aligns with your season, your calling, and your capacity.

https://dawnmrivers.com/start

You do not have to walk the next phase alone. In fact, this work was never meant to be done in isolation. Healing is powerful, yes, but healing in community, with guidance and structure, becomes generational.

There are several ways to continue your journey, each designed to support a different phase of your Spiral:

The Luxe Flow Society

For women craving ongoing support, sisterhood, and spiritually aligned growth.

This is where you plug into community, receive monthly teachings, access live discussions, and continue integrating your inner shifts with consistency and ease. Think of it as your spiritual gym. The place you return to for alignment, accountability, and elevation.

Awakened Woman Academy

For the woman who is ready for structured transformation with guidance, depth, and momentum.

The Awakened Woman Academy is a guided, six-month immersive experience designed to help you move from awareness into embodiment. This is where the inner work becomes integrated, where insight turns into practice, and where identity begins to shift in real time. Inside the Academy, you will work through the foundational teachings of the Spiral with intention and structure, supported by curriculum, reflection, and live guidance. This is not passive learning. It is active becoming. If you know you are ready to stop circling the same patterns and want a clear, supported path forward without the intensity of private coaching but with the support of a group, this is where your next evolution takes root.

VIP Days

For the woman ready for an intensive transformation.

These private, high-touch sessions collapse months of work into one sacred, immersive experience. You and I go deep into your narrative, your patterns, your lineage, and your next identity. It's potent. It's powerful. It's identity surgery for the woman standing on the edge of her next evolution.

1:1 Coaching

For the woman who knows she needs a personal guide.

This container is intimate, soulful, strategic, and deeply supportive. You'll move through the deeper layers of your generational story, heal the patterns that still grip you, and rise into a version of yourself you haven't yet fully met. This is for the woman who is ready to transform from the inside out.

The Luxe Identity Spiral™ Certification

For the woman who feels the call to lead.

This is a training and it's an initiation. You will learn the full Spiral system, master the emotional and generational tools, and become a certified facilitator capable of guiding others through their own awakenings. If your soul is whispering that you are meant to help other women rise, this is your path.

You don't have to decide today. You simply get to choose what feels aligned, available, and honest for who you are right now.

Whatever your next step is, know this: I am holding space for you. I am cheering for you. And I am honored to walk beside you as you rise into the woman your lineage has been waiting for.

https://dawnmrivers.com/start

FREE RESOURCES AND NEXT STEPS

Your journey doesn't end at the final page of this book. In many ways, it's the beginning. Transformation is not a one-time realization; it is an ongoing relationship with your identity, your lineage, and your future.

To support you as you continue rising through your own spiral of becoming, I've created a space where you can access additional guidance, tools, teachings, and community; all in one place.

Welcome to The Luxe Resource Lounge.

Inside this online hub, you'll find a curated collection of free offerings designed to meet you exactly where you are in your evolution. Whether you are beginning your journey, deepening your self-awareness, or preparing to lead at your next level, the Lounge will grow with you.

This space includes guides, checklists, meditations, assessments, tutorials, and teaching videos that expand on the themes you explored in this book; all grounded in my years of study, teaching, and coaching in identity work, yoga philosophy, and transformational frameworks.

You'll have access to practices that support nervous system regulation and reconnection to your inner wisdom; tools to help you integrate identity shifts and rewrite old narratives; and Spiral-based assessments to help you understand your patterns and map your next steps.

This is not about temporary inspiration; it is about sustained transformation and embodiment.

Over time, the Lounge will continue to evolve with new tools, classes, workshops, and teachings to support your ongoing growth. Consider it your home base, your starting point for deeper alignment; and your anchor for every next-level version of yourself.

To access the Lounge, simply visit the link provided below. Once inside, you'll also find ways to connect with the community, explore deeper support, and stay informed about upcoming opportunities.

Your journey continues. Let these resources support your expansion at every step.

https://dawnmrivers.com/lounge

Bulk Orders

You Get What You Get is available for bulk purchase for book clubs, corporate wellness programs, women's organizations, sororities, retreats, conferences, and speaking engagements.

Discounted pricing is available for orders of 10 or more copies.

Bulk orders make powerful gifts for teams, communities, and the women in your life who are ready to break cycles and reclaim their identity.

To inquire about bulk pricing, customized orders, or having Dawn speak at your event, visit:

dawnmrivers.com/contact

Closing Reflection

As you reach the final words of this book, I want to return to where my own journey began, with my mother. Her story shaped me long before I ever had language for generational patterns or the courage to question them. She gave me strength, resilience, creativity, and determination. She also handed down wounds, fears, and expectations that were never meant to be mine. And like many daughters, I carried both without knowing the difference.

It has taken years, decades, to untangle what belonged to my lineage and what belonged to my becoming. It has taken courage to acknowledge the pain I inherited. Compassion to rewrite what I once judged. And patience to forgive the patterns that shaped her before they ever touched me.

But this is the legacy of a cycle-breaker.

You honor what was.
You heal what hurts.
You choose what continues.
You release what must end.

My children will never fully understand the cycles I ended so they could begin differently. They won't know the tears that softened me, the boundaries that protected me, the identities I outgrew, or the truth I fought to reclaim. They will simply inherit the freedom. And that is enough.

This is my legacy: not perfection, not a flawless lineage, but a conscious one. A lineage built with intention, awareness, and love. A lineage where truth is allowed, mistakes are repaired, and emotional safety is practiced, not assumed.

And now I offer the same possibility to you:

Become the ancestor your descendants will thank. Become the one who chooses a higher path. Become the woman who interrupts centuries of silence with one brave decision to heal.

You have everything you need to begin.
You have a framework.
You have tools.You have clarity.

Most importantly, you have a lineage waiting for its turning point, and you are it.

The Spiral continues.
Your legacy awaits.

Epilogue

When my mother died, she gave me a gift.

For eight years, my mother told me she wanted to die. Hearing it over and over made me angry. I felt betrayed. I believed that if I stayed, if I cared for her, something would shift. I hoped she would impart wisdom to me and to her grandchildren. I hoped our relationship would heal. I hoped she would want to live again, even if only in small, ordinary ways.

None of that happened.

After two years of living in her home, I no longer felt like her daughter. I felt like "the help." I had one room. One shelf in the pantry. Almost no say in what we watched or listened to. I was present, but never fully included.

Eventually, I told her I was leaving.

She came to my room and said, "Please don't leave me."

I stayed. I told her things needed to change because I was unhappy.

They barely changed.

I remained unhappy. Every attempt I made to do something new with her was met with resistance. The resentment between us became palpable. I know she felt it, as deeply as I did.

One day she said, "We used to be friends."

I answered, "We were never friends. I only did everything you told me to do."

I wanted to be seen. I wanted to be heard. I wanted to be loved. I longed for the kind of relationship I saw my friends have with their mothers. When I realized that was not possible with my own, I invested more deeply in my relationship with my stepmother. I visited her in Chicago a few times a year. She was affectionate and present. I admired her deeply. After a devastating accident that fractured vertebrae in her neck, doctors told her she would never walk again. She proved them wrong.

I wanted that kind of will for my mother, too. She was only twenty-two years older than me.

My wishes never came true.

As her health declined, I tried to move her into assisted living. I toured facilities. I took her to one. I attempted to take her to others, only to have her refuse to get dressed or leave the house. After two years of resistance, I stopped trying. She had fired caregivers. Canceled doctor appointments. Withdrawn from her remaining friends.

Near the end, she spoke very little. She barely ate. She rarely bathed. She sat in her chair for hours, detached from the world.

A few weeks before she died, I told my best friend and my cousin that I didn't believe my mother had much time left. Something wasn't right.

Right before I was scheduled for a four-day flying trip, I told her we were going to the doctor when I returned. She insisted her medication was the problem. She said her concierge doctor would see her the following month. I told her that wasn't good enough.

I asked where her Life Alert was. She said it was upstairs on her bedpost. I brought it down and asked her to wear it. Her breathing didn't sound right to me.

Three days later, emergency services called. My mother had fallen off the couch and couldn't get up. EMS was dispatched. I called my neighbor and asked her to meet them at the house. My mother insisted she was fine. I asked that she be taken to the hospital. Because she was cognizant, they needed my power of attorney paperwork. My neighbor retrieved it and gave it to the paramedics.

That was Sunday, November 30, 2025.

Once she was admitted, I called to tell her I wouldn't be home until after midnight but would come immediately if she wanted me to. She told me to come in the morning.

When I arrived the next day, she didn't look right. Her complexion had turned slightly green. She was not herself. The care team told me she had a urinary tract infection and explained that patients over seventy can experience extreme behavioral changes.

I was uneasy with that explanation and asked for additional testing.

Meanwhile, social workers and physical therapists began discussing rehabilitation placement. That wasn't possible. I was in the process of moving, and no one would be home to care for her. She knew this. I had told her weeks earlier that I was actively searching for an apartment across town.

Then I left for another four-day trip. I was anxious and deeply unsettled. I expressed my concern repeatedly. She was marked as a fall risk but kept trying to get out of bed. They knew she had heart failure. They knew she had fallen multiple times over the previous two years. They knew no home care agency was involved.

I was overwhelmed.

On Thursday, December 4, at 4:45 a.m., I received a call in my Chicago hotel room. My mother had suffered a stroke. She couldn't speak but was stable. A CT scan was ordered. Later, they confirmed it was a massive stroke affecting multiple areas of her brain, caused by her heart condition.

I booked a flight back to Cleveland immediately.

By the time I arrived, she could only whisper the word "no." When I entered her room, she reached for me, struggling to speak. Her vision had deteriorated. She could no longer track where people where in the room.

"I'm here, Mom," I said, and took her hand.

She declined rapidly after that. She lost the ability to swallow. She grew weaker by the hour. Because of her advanced directives, she could not receive IV fluids, feeding tubes, or aggressive medication. She was transferred to hospice care.

When my daughter Brittany arrived on Saturday, my mother was gasping for air. It was the most horrific thing I have ever witnessed. She was in pain. Her body had begun shutting down. She could no longer respond.

After six hours of labored breathing, she died on Sunday, December 7, 2025.

She was gone within a week.

And it was a gift.

She released me.

I was finally able to move forward without fear, without guilt, without carrying the weight of her choices as my responsibility.

Thank you, Mom.

I forgive you

I'm sorry.

I love you.

Afterword

YOU GET WHAT YOU GET BECAUSE YOU GET WHO YOU ARE

I wanted to name this book *You Get What You Get Because You Get Who You Are.*

It's a phrase I say often. It's become known as a *Dawnism*. And while it may sound simple, it carries a layered truth that has guided my life and my work.

The phrase is rooted in three traditions often confused with one another: the biblical idea of reaping what you sow, the Law of Attraction, and karma. They are related, but they are not the same.

Reaping and sowing is about consequence and harvest. When you plant a seed, you don't receive the seed back. You receive the multiplication of that seed. One kernel of corn does not return as one kernel. It becomes a stalk, with ears of corn, each containing hundreds of kernels. What you plant grows beyond what you expect.

Karma, however, is not punishment.

Karma is the clearing of samskaras, the mental impressions and habitual patterns formed by every thought, intention, and action. These impressions live in the body, the subconscious, and the soul. They shape behavior, belief, and destiny. In yogic philosophy, you cannot reach liberation while carrying unexamined residue. Karma gives you opportunities to clear it.

I came to understand karma as a forgiveness cycle. Like the rinse cycle of a washing machine, it exists to remove what remains after the first pass. You can run it again if needed. My mother used to rinse her clothes twice because her skin was sensitive. She could always tell when residue was left behind.

Karma works the same way. You are given more than one chance to clean your life.

The Law of Attraction operates differently. It is not about reward or correction. It is about resonance.

Like energy attracts like energy. Your inner frequency shapes your outer reality.

But this is not about fake positivity or affirmations spoken without embodiment. It is about energetic truth.

In the Spiral, we teach that attraction is rooted in alignment, not perfection. You do not attract what you want. You attract who you are.

Your energy speaks louder than your words. You can call yourself a coach all day, but if you are not living as one, the world will reflect that truth back to you. You cannot think your way into a new life. You must become the frequency of the life you are calling in.

If you want aligned relationships, become aligned.
If you want abundance, embody overflow.
If you want clients, become coachable.

This work is not about pretending.
It is about becoming.

And that is why, in the end, the truth still stands:

    You get what you get
    because you get
    who you are.

Acknowledgements

The seed of this book was planted in 2017 by Chrystal McNeal, my former elementary school colleague. She saw in me something I never thought I would or could do: write a book. She would tell me that I was going to write a book and I repeatedly said, "No I'm not."

As you can see, she was right. Thank you, Chrystal.

To my beautiful, intelligent, brave children, Brittany and Brenton, who have been my biggest supporters and encouragers since I decided to do things differently in 2012. Thank you for allowing me to be your mother.

To my ride-or-die best friend Jasmine, thank you for the suggestion to study my birth chart. For days and days, I studied my sun, moon, and rising. Then for months I read countless books and endlessly listened to new podcasts that supported this anthropological study I had begun. I journaled and cried until something new was born. Out of that intense work came my Soul Blueprint and then The Luxe Identity Spiral.

To the Wellness Gang, Gang, Gang for being with me from yoga studio ownership to now published author. You are my Mastermind Sisters. From special events, to retreats, to strategic planning, to spilling soup, to an epic Dawntember dance party! I love you all so much.

To my early readers, Monica and Shelley. To my supportive blurb writers: Marissa A. Nance, Dr. Sanaa Jaman, Keisean Raines, Tara Pringle Jefferson, Annette L. Hollimon, Tenora Edwards, Sianna Sherman, Nike Olabisi-Green, and Ylonda Rosenthal-Greene.

To the Luxe Launch Ambassadors for supporting me and this book by connecting me with your networks and sharing my work near and far. I am beyond grateful.

To the best neighbors anyone could ever have, the Maloneys. Thank you for looking after my mom whenever I was away from home, for being members of the Daybreak Yoga studio community, for shoveling the driveway, for taking out the trash, for listening to me vent, and so much more. I'm indebted to you.

To the flight crews who gave me space to write this book on the plane, talk about it endlessly, and share what I was doing with anyone who would listen, I'm truly grateful.

To all my yoga students, mentees, team members, and coaching clients, thank you for trusting me to lead you on this journey.

And to you, dear reader, thank you for finishing the book. For the dog-earred pages, highlights, and notes in the margins. For sharing Dawnisms and quotes on social media. For gifting the book to your friends and family. For seeing yourself in the stories I shared. It's all because of you.

Notes

The books referenced throughout this work are listed by chapter for your convenience.

To explore these titles further, visit:

dawnmrivers.com/amazon

This page contains affiliate links. Dawn M. Rivers may earn a small commission from qualifying purchases at no additional cost to you.

Introduction

Meyer, Joyce. *Battlefield of the Mind: Winning the Battle in Your Mind*. New York: FaithWords, 1995.

Chapter 2

Adele, Deborah. *The Yamas & Niyamas: Exploring Yoga's Ethical Practice*. Duluth, MN: On-Word Bound Books, 2009.

Cascio, Christopher N., Matthew Brook O'Donnell, Francis J. Tinney, Matthew D. Lieberman, Shelley E. Taylor, Victor J. Strecher, and Emily B. Falk. "Self-Affirmation Activates Brain Systems Associated with Self-Related Processing and Reward and Is Reinforced by Future Orientation." *Social Cognitive and Affective Neuroscience* 11, no. 4 (2016): 621–629.

DeGruy, Joy. *Post Traumatic Slave Syndrome: America's Legacy of Enduring Injury and Healing*. Portland, OR: Uptone Press, 2005.

Hanson, Rick. *Buddha's Brain: The Practical Neuroscience of Happiness, Love, and Wisdom*. Oakland: New Harbinger Publications, 2009.

Lazar, Sara W., Catherine E. Kerr, Rachel H. Wasserman, Jeremy R. Gray, Douglas N. Greve, Michael T. Treadway, Metta McGarvey, Brian T. Quinn, Jeffery A. Dusek, Herbert Benson, Scott L. Rauch, Christopher I. Moore, and Bruce

Fischl. "Meditation Experience Is Associated with Increased Cortical Thickness." *NeuroReport* 16, no. 17 (2005): 1893–1897.

Mulligan, Connie J., Edward B. Quinn, Dima Hamadmad, Christopher L. Dutton, Lisa Nevell, Alexandra M. Binder, Catherine Panter-Brick, and Rana Dajani. "Epigenetic Signatures of Intergenerational Exposure to Violence in Three Generations of Syrian Refugees." *Scientific Reports* 15, no. 1 (2025): 5945.

Yehuda, Rachel, Nikolaos P. Daskalakis, Linda M. Bierer, Heather N. Bader, Torsten Klengel, Florian Holsboer, and Elisabeth B. Binder. "Holocaust Exposure Induced Intergenerational Effects on FKBP5 Methylation." *Biological Psychiatry* 80, no. 5 (2016): 372–380.

Chapter 4

Warren, Rick. *The Purpose Driven Life: What on Earth Am I Here For?* Grand Rapids, MI: Zondervan, 2002.

Chapter 5

Williamson, Marianne. *A Return to Love: Reflections on the Principles of* A Course in Miracles. New York: HarperCollins, 1992.

Chapter 8

Webb, Koya. *Let Your Fears Make You Fierce: How to Turn Common Obstacles into a Fearless Life.* Carlsbad, CA: Hay House, 2019.

About the Author

Dawn M. Rivers is a transformational life coach, speaker, and author whose work explores the intersections of identity, alignment, generational patterns, and personal transformation.

A certified yoga teacher with over two decades of study and teaching experience, she created the Luxe Identity Spiral™ framework, informed by insights from neuroscience, epigenetics, and yoga philosophy, to help women identify inherited patterns, understand the conditioning shaping their choices, and intentionally create lives that feel aligned, fulfilling, and their own.

She is the founder of DMR Coaching & Consulting and the creator of the Luxe Flow Society.

Dawn lives her work out loud; and yes, much of this book was written at 35,000 feet.

Learn more at dawnmrivers.com.